Catch A Falling Star:
A Guided Journal for Single Moms Who Want to Live Life, Love, and Parent Successfully

This journal belongs
to:

ISBN: 978-1-953697-25-7 (Paperback)
ISBN: 978-1-953697-26-4 (Hardcover)
ISBN: 978-1-953697-27-1 (Ebook)
Library of Congress Control Number: 2023911630

Written by Rikkianisha Hunt

Printed by Amazon and IngramSpark in the United States of America.

First printing edition 2023.

Asante Publishing, LLC
8170 Mall Parkway #1614
Lithonia, GA 30038
www.asantepublishing.com

To my little twinkle, my son, Mason, this book is dedicated to you. You are my guiding star, the light that illuminates my path. I do this for you, my love, to create a better world and a brighter future.

How to Use this Journal

STAR GUIDE

Work through the journal at your own pace. Use these icons to guide you through the exercises.
You will need a pen, star stickers and crayons or colored pencils.

POSITIVE AFFIRMATION

Stand in front of a mirror, take a cleansing deep breath, repeat the affirmation 3 times, take another cleansing deep breath.

INSPIRATION

- Read and Reflect
- Letters of Support
- Star Advice

WRITING ACTIVITY

- Goal Setting
- Practice Your Gratitude
- Written in the Stars
- Journal Prompts

STICKERS

- Give yourself credit for a job well done
- Sunday Self-Care Bingo (First complete a row or column/vertical, horizontal or diagonal. then see if you can cover the entire card)

COLOR

Use crayons or colored pencils.

- Wellness Wheel
- Coloring Pages

Intro

Hello, Star,

I wrote this journal with you in mind. I recognize that you're carrying the weight of the world on your shoulders, often without the support you truly deserve. Your journey as a single mom can often lead to feelings of fatigue, guilt, social and physical isolation, and financial insecurity. You feel the absence of a helping hand when you need it most. These are all valid struggles. Maintaining housing, childcare, and employment all while providing a healthy and happy environment for your child is a challenge but YOU CAN DO IT! Let me tell you, dear star, you shine brighter than you realize.

Whether you feel like you're falling or have already fallen, it is never too late to rise, to ascend to greater heights, and to reach for the heavens. You hold the power within yourself to catch a falling star—you don't need to wait for anyone else to do it for you. My love, it's time to catch yourself!

At the core of it all, you are the central figure. You cannot be the best mother to your children if you are constantly falling and flickering. Self-care is not just important; it is essential. So, carve out some precious moments in your day—early mornings before the chaos begins, or late nights after the kids have drifted off to sleep. Dedicate 15 to 30 minutes to work through this guided journal.

Take this opportunity to assess each area of your life, to carefully examine where you can improve the quality of your experiences. Remember, you are the architect of your own happiness, and by actively participating in crafting a plan, you pave the way for a brighter future. Let the journal be your companion as you chart a course toward a life filled with joy, love, and success. Believe in yourself, dear moms, and watch as the stars align in your favor.

Within these pages, you will find exercises designed to help you build the support system you need to truly sparkle and shine. It won't be easy, but I know you are capable of embracing the challenges and transforming them into triumphs. You are stronger than you think, and I believe in you with all my heart.

Let this journal be your companion on this journey of self-discovery and growth. Write down your thoughts, dreams, and desires. Explore your fears and find the courage to face them. Set goals, big or small, and take steps towards making them a reality. Reflect on your blessings, celebrate your strengths, and learn from your experiences.

Remember, dear star, you are not alone. There are others out there who understand your struggles and are willing to support you. As you embark on this guided journaling adventure, may you uncover the radiance within your soul, ignite your passions, and find the strength to embrace life, love, and successfully parent.
You can do it, my dear star. I have faith in you, and I am here cheering you on every step of the way.

With love and unwavering support,

Rikki

Wellness Wheel

The Wellness Wheel is a coaching tool that helps you understand exactly what it is that you want to change in your life. It allows you to see what your life consists of now and what is really important to you. Take a close look at the wheel segments and assess each of them. Now rate the current state of each segment from 1 to 10 points (1 for very dissatisfied, 10 for completely satisfied) and **color the segment accordingly**. Once completed, your wheel will help you see where changes can positively affect your whole life.

Love (RED): Are your needs for love and intimacy being met? Is the affection that you give being reciprocated? In your romantic or sexual relationships, do you choose partner(s) who respect your wants, needs, and choices? Are you satisfied with your level of physical intimacy, to include: displays of affection and sexual acts with a partner? Are you satisfied with your level of emotional intimacy?

Work (ORANGE): Do you get personal satisfaction and enrichment from work? Do you believe that you are able to contribute your knowledge, skills, and talents at work? Do you seek out opportunities to improve your knowledge or skills? Do you balance your social life and job responsibilities well? Do you effectively handle your level of stress related to work responsibilities? Is your workload manageable? Have you explored paid and/or volunteer opportunities that interest you?

Spiritual (YELLOW): Do you know who you are, what you value, where you fit in, and where you're going? Do you engage in acts of caring and goodwill without expecting something in return? Are your values reflected in your actions? Do you feel connected to something larger than yourself? (e.g., God, higher power, nature, connectedness of all living things, humanity, community?) Do you feel like your life has purpose and meaning?

Finances (GREEN): Do you have a good handle on your financial status? Do you have money on hand to meet current expenses? Do you understand the issues of balancing your wants and needs, and balancing saving and spending? Do you have money on hand or available credit to deal with moderate unexpected life expenses such as a needed car repair, broken glasses, or an emergency trip? Do you pay your bills on time, and rarely or never get overdue notices, over-limit fees, or bounced check notices? Do you check your credit reports at least once a year? Are your savings aligned with your life goals, such as home ownership, educating your children, or retirement? Do you worry about money?

Wellness Wheel

Mental (BLUE): Do you find it easy to express your emotions in positive, constructive ways? Do you recognize when you are stressed and take steps to manage your stress (e.g., exercise, quiet time, meditation, or counseling)? Are you resilient and able to bounce back after a disappointment or problem? When angry, do you let others know in non-confrontational or non-hurtful ways? Are you overwhelmed with stress, traumatic experiences, mental illness or addiction? Do you experience joy and laughter?

Health (PURPLE): Do you engage in physical exercise regularly (e.g., 30 mins at least 3-5 times a week?) Do you get 6-8 hours of sleep each night? Do you abstain from drinking alcohol; or drink in moderation with no negative consequences such as DUI, blackouts, or unsafe behaviors while drinking? Do you avoid using tobacco products or other drugs? Do you eat a balanced diet (fruits, vegetables, low-moderate fat, whole grains)? Do you get regular physical exams and dental visits?

Kids (AQUA): Is your child well-adjusted? Are you able to set limits and stick to them? Are you able to discipline or correct without yelling or physical punishment? Are you able to laugh and play with your child? Do you show love and affection? Does your child come to you when hurt or facing a problem? Does your child have a healthy relationship with their other parent/guardian or are they adjusting well to the absence of a parent/guardian?

Social Support (PINK): Do you feel supported and respected in your close relationships? Do you have a support network of other single moms or parents who can relate to your experiences? Are there individuals in your life who offer practical help or assistance when you need it? Do you participate in activities and social events that allow you opportunities to form new relationships? Are there any community resources or support groups that you are aware of and utilize? Do you feel a sense of belonging in your community?

When setting your goals, visualize a fully colored wheel, a balanced life. Consider what changes will lead you to live your BEST life. What goals can you set and what plans can you make in the next 30 days?

Wellness Wheel

THE WELLNESS WHEEL IS A GREAT TOOL THAT HELPS
YOU BETTER UNDERSTAND WHAT YOU CAN DO TO
MAKE YOUR LIFE MORE BALANCED. THINK ABOUT
THE 8 LIFE CATEGORIES BELOW, AND RATE THEM
FROM 1 - 10.

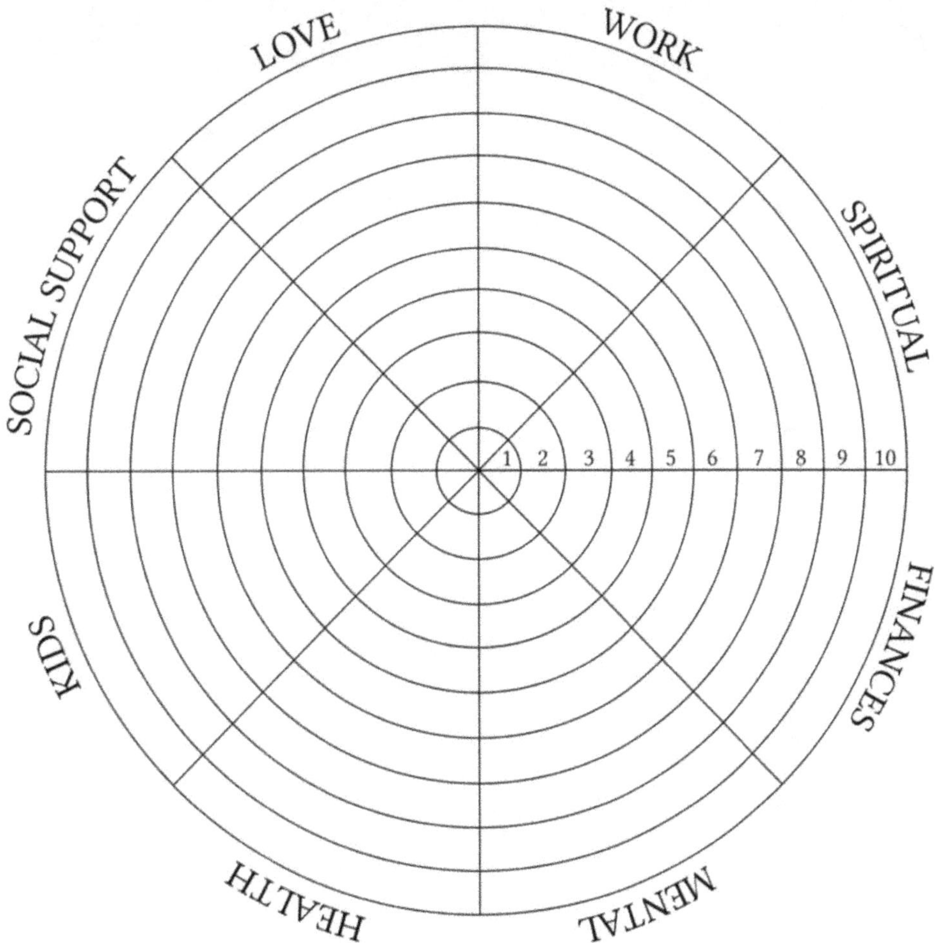

Love (Red), Work (Orange), Spiritual (Yellow), Finances (Green), Mental (BLUE), Health (Purple), Kids (Aqua),
Social Support (Pink)

WE ARE ALL OF US
STARS, AND WE
DESERVE TO
TWINKLE
.~MARILYN MONROE

STAR BREATHING

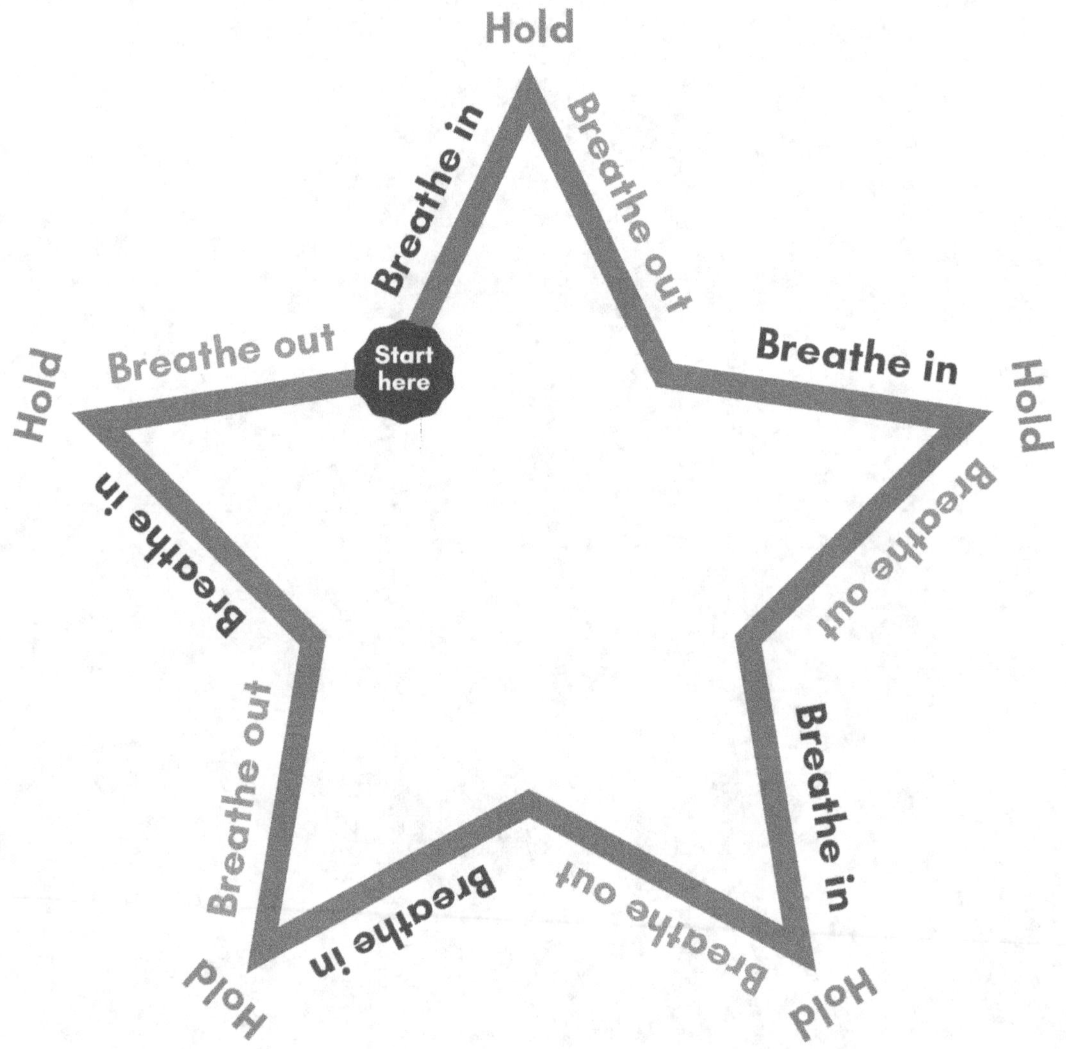

Trace your finger up one side of the star, while you take a deep breath in. Hold your breath at the point and breathe out as you slide down the other side. Keep going until you've gone around the whole star.

I can do this

Written in the Stars

Written in the Stars

A Falling
Star
Still
Shines.
~Tablo

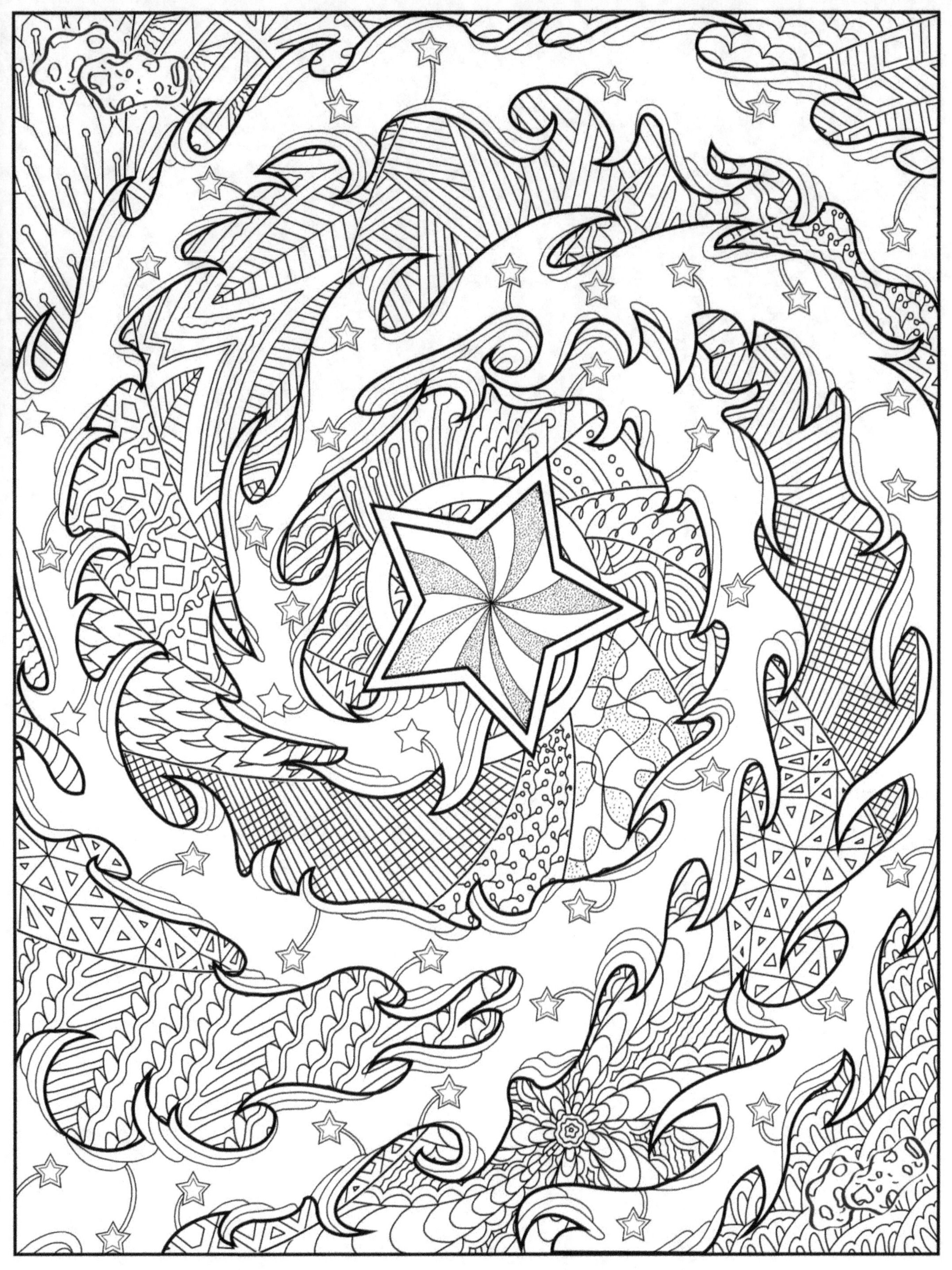

PRACTICE
YOUR
GRATITUDE

WHAT AM I GRATEFUL FOR?

Love

Finding Love Among the Stars

Dear Single Moms

In the vast tapestry of the night sky, amidst the shimmering stars that light up the darkness, there is a message of hope that I wish to share with you today. It is a message that speaks of love, resilience, and the possibility of finding love again, regardless of the circumstances that led you to be single. Whether it be widowhood, separation, divorce, or a conscious choice to prioritize your journey, I want to encourage you to embrace the beauty of love and to never wall off your heart.

Just as stars illuminate the night, love has the power to illuminate our lives with joy, connection, and fulfillment. It may feel like an impossible dream in the midst of the challenges and responsibilities you face as a single mom, but I want you to know that love is possible for you. You deserve to experience the deep connection and affection that a loving partnership can bring.

It is understandable that when faced with the trials of single parenthood, the instinct to go into survival mode and believe you must do everything on your own can be strong. But, dear single moms, I urge you not to let that mindset close your heart off from the possibility of love. You are capable of so much, and embracing love does not mean you are weak or incapable. On the contrary, opening your heart to love is a courageous act that can bring immeasurable joy and support to your life.

Just as stars are born from the remnants of previous stars, our capacity to love is resilient and ever-renewing. You have loved before, and even if that love has changed or ended, it does not mean that love will not find its way back into your life. Your experiences have shaped you, made you stronger, and prepared you for the love that lies ahead.

Love, dear single moms, knows no boundaries of age, circumstance, or past. It has a way of finding us when we least expect it, and sometimes when we need it the most. Allow yourself to heal, to grow, and to find solace in your journey as a single mom. And when the time is right, when your heart whispers that it is ready, be open to the possibility of love once again.

Remember, you are deserving of love, companionship, and a partner who will walk beside you on this beautiful path of life. Love does not diminish your strength; it enhances it. It adds depth, joy, and a sense of belonging that can nourish your soul and enrich your children's lives.

So, dear single moms, as you navigate the challenges and triumphs of your unique journey, hold onto the hope that love is not lost to you. The stars in the night sky remind us that even in the darkest hours, there is always a glimmer of light, a promise of something beautiful yet to come.

Keep your heart open to the possibilities, embrace the love that awaits you, and trust that the universe has a plan for your happiness. You are not alone in this journey. Love will find its way to you when the time is right. May the stars above guide you towards a future filled with love, happiness, and the warmth of a loving partner.

With unwavering support,

Rikki.

Dating as a Single Mom:

1. Self-Reflection: Before diving into the dating world, take time for self-reflection. Understand your own needs, values, and priorities in a relationship. This self-awareness will guide you in finding a partner who is compatible and supportive.
2. Open Communication: When starting to date someone, be open and transparent about being a single mom. Share your responsibilities and the role your children play in your life. This will help potential partners understand your situation and decide if they are ready for a committed relationship with a single parent.
3. Seek therapy or counseling: Sometimes, past traumas or relationship patterns can affect our ability to form and maintain healthy connections.

Star Advice

Introducing Someone New to Your Kids:

- Timing is Key: Introducing someone new to your children is a significant step. Take your time to build a strong foundation with your partner before involving your children. It's important to ensure the relationship has potential for long-term commitment.
- Honest Conversation: Have an open and age-appropriate conversation with your children about your decision to introduce someone new. Assure them that they are still your priority and that their feelings are valid. Address any concerns they may have and provide reassurance.
- Casual and Comfortable Setting: Choose a relaxed and familiar environment for the initial meeting between your children and your partner. This can help alleviate tension and create a comfortable atmosphere for everyone involved.
- Slow and Steady: Allow the relationship between your partner and your children to develop naturally. Encourage shared activities and quality time together, but also respect the need for individual connections to form over time.

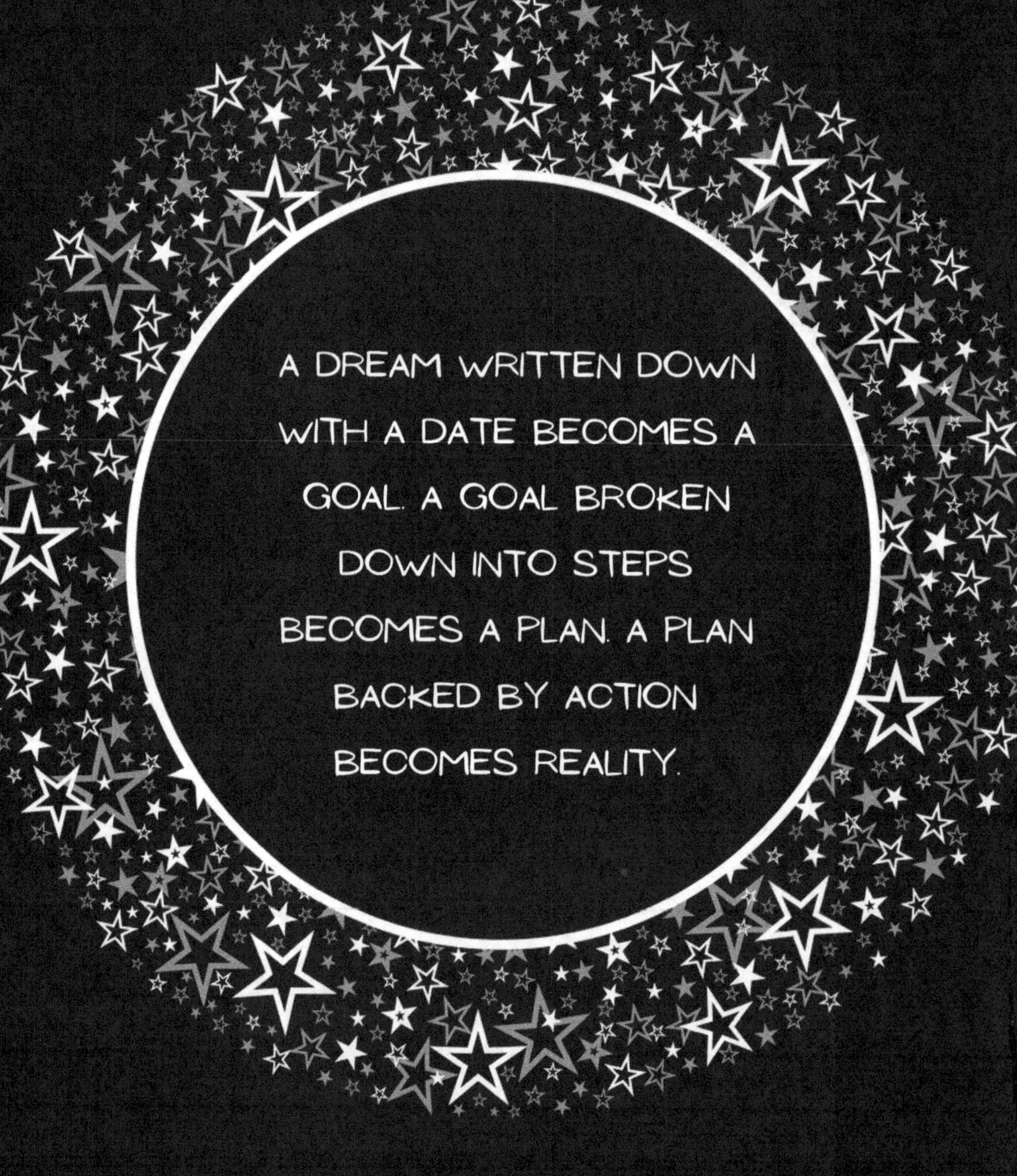
A DREAM WRITTEN DOWN
WITH A DATE BECOMES A
GOAL. A GOAL BROKEN
DOWN INTO STEPS
BECOMES A PLAN. A PLAN
BACKED BY ACTION
BECOMES REALITY.

LOVE

WHY IS THIS IMPORTANT FOR ME?

____

____

____

____

ACTION STEPS

ROAD BLOCK

01 ___________________________________

02 ___________________________________

03 ___________________________________

04 ___________________________________

05 ___________________________________

06 ___________________________________

07 ___________________________________

08 ___________________________________

09 ___________________________________

10 ___________________________________

START DATE

END DATE

NOTES

BRILLIANT
AND
BRIGHT

When I am ready
for love,
it will find me.

Written in the Stars

SUGGESTIONS:

- LETTER TO YOUR YOUNGER SELF
- LETTER TO YOUR FUTURE SELF
- LETTER TO YOUR CHILDREN
- LETTER OF FORGIVENESS
- LETTER OF APOLOGY
- JOURNAL

Written in the Stars

I welcome healthy
relationships.

Strength in Vulnerability:

Write about a time when you opened up and allowed yourself to be
vulnerable. How did this vulnerability connect you with others?

____
____
____
____
____
____
____
____
____
____
____
____
____

New Beginnings:

Envision a fresh start in an area of your life. What steps can you take to embrace change and welcome new beginnings?

I AM
POWERFUL
GENUINE
INCREDIBLE
TENACIOUS
BOLD
AMAZING
INTELLIGENT
MIGHTY
COURAGEOUS
RESILIENT
VALUABLE
BRAVE
MOTIVATED
UNIQUE
IMPORTANT
RESOURCEFUL
NEEDED
SUCCESSFUL
AWESOME
WORTHY
EMPOWERED
STRONG
SUPPORTIVE
FIERCE
FEARLESS
CAPABLE

PRACTICE
YOUR
GRATITUDE

WHAT AM I GRATEFUL FOR?

Work

Star Advice

Finding a fulfilling career that provides financial security, and personal satisfaction:

- Assess current employment situation: Evaluate job satisfaction, growth opportunities, and alignment with long-term goals.
- Enhance skills and qualifications: Identify areas for improvement and seek professional development opportunities.
- Explore flexible work options: Research jobs that offer flexibility to balance work and parenting responsibilities.
- Network and seek support: Connect with professional networks and seek mentorship or guidance.

WORK

01

02

03

04

05

06

07

08

09

10

START
DATE

END
DATE

STAY INSPIRED

Time Mastery:

Describe a time-management challenge you face as a single mom. How can you streamline your schedule to create more balance and quality time?

____

____

____

____

____

____

____

____

____

____

____

____

____

★ ★ ★ ★ ★

I am so
proud of
you.

Written in the Stars

Written in the Stars

Setting Intentions:

Craft a mantra for yourself, aligned with your aspirations as a single mom. How can repeating this mantra positively impact your mindset?

____

____

____

____

____

____

____

____

____

____

____

____

Life's Constellations:

Describe a challenge you overcame that has shaped your journey. How has this experience contributed to your growth as both a person and a parent?

Goal
digger

PRACTICE
YOUR
GRATITUDE

WHAT AM I GRATEFUL FOR?

Star Advice

Spiritual well-being that provides guidance, strength, and a sense of purpose:

- Reflect on your spiritual beliefs: Explore and define what spirituality means to you.
- Practice mindfulness and meditation: Incorporate daily practices to connect with your inner self.
- Engage in spiritual communities: Join groups or organizations that align with your beliefs for support and connection.
- Seek spiritual guidance: Consider seeking guidance from mentors, counselors, or religious leaders.

SPIRITUAL

01

02

03

04

05

06

07

08

09

10

START
DATE

END
DATE

Your light is needed. Never let anyone dull your sparkle

I am the Mom
that God
chose me to be.

STAR BREATHING

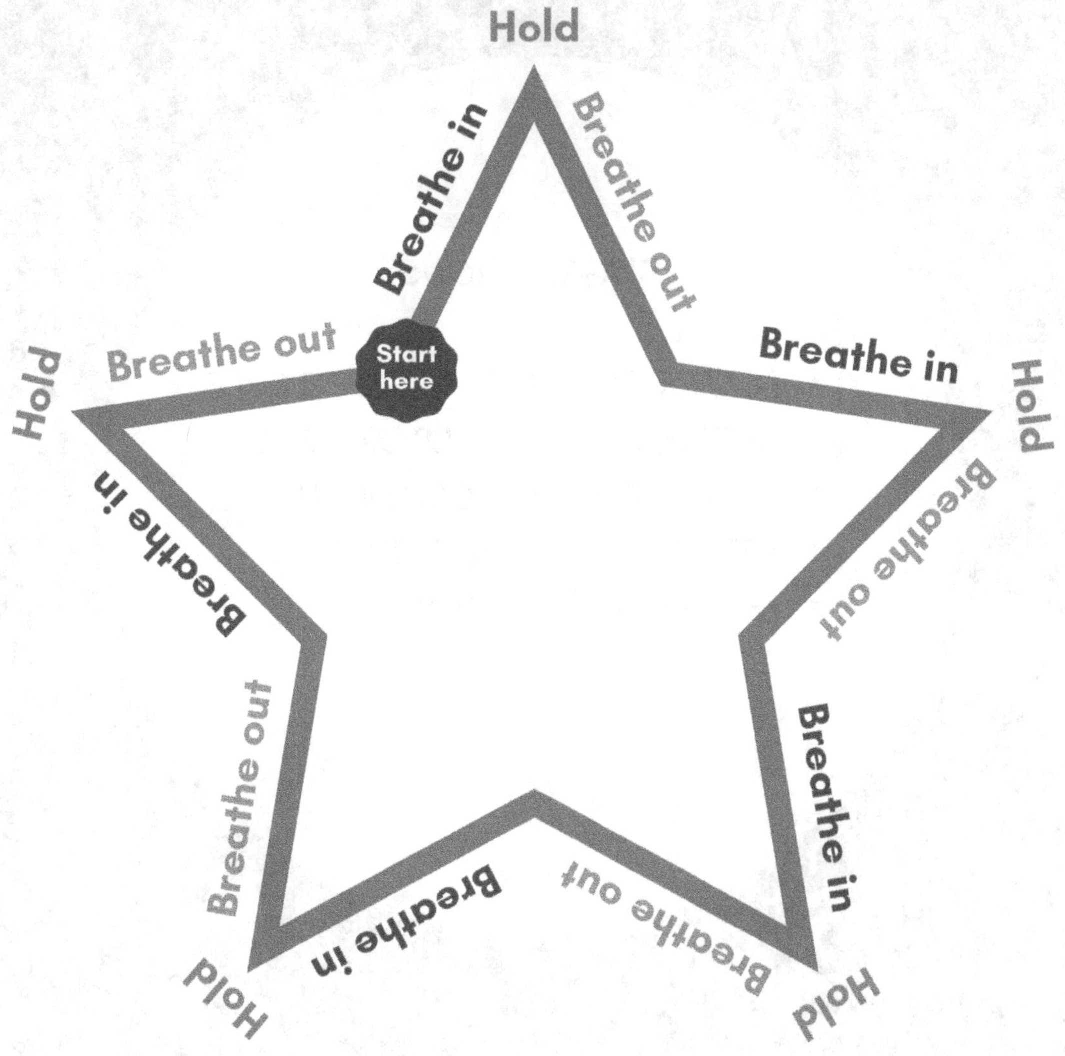

Trace your finger up one side of the star, while you take a deep breath in. Hold your breath at the point and breathe out as you slide down the other side. Keep going until you've gone around the whole star.

Written in the Stars

SUGGESTIONS:

• LETTER TO YOUR YOUNGER SELF
• LETTER TO YOUR FUTURE SELF
• LETTER TO YOUR CHILDREN
• LETTER OF FORGIVENESS
• LETTER OF APOLOGY
• JOURNAL

Written in the Stars

Claiming Your Strengths:

List five qualities that make you an exceptional mom.

THINGS TO REMEMBER
Tommorow is a new day
Making mistakes is a part of life
Saying 'No' is okay
Not everyone has to like you
Beauty & strength come from within

I am beautiful,
inside and out.

Star

PRACTICE
YOUR
GRATITUDE

WHAT AM I GRATEFUL FOR?

Finances

Achieve financial stability
and create a secure future
for yourself and your children

- Assess current financial situation: Review income, expenses, debts, and savings.
- Create a budget: Develop a realistic budget that includes savings and identifies areas for potential cutbacks.
- Increase income sources: Explore opportunities for additional income, such as part-time work or freelancing.
- Seek financial assistance and resources: Research programs, grants, and support available for single mothers.

FINANCES

____

____

____

01 ____________________________

02 ____________________________

03 ____________________________

04 ____________________________

05 ____________________________

06 ____________________________

07 ____________________________

08 ____________________________

09 ____________________________

10 ____________________________

START
DATE

END
DATE

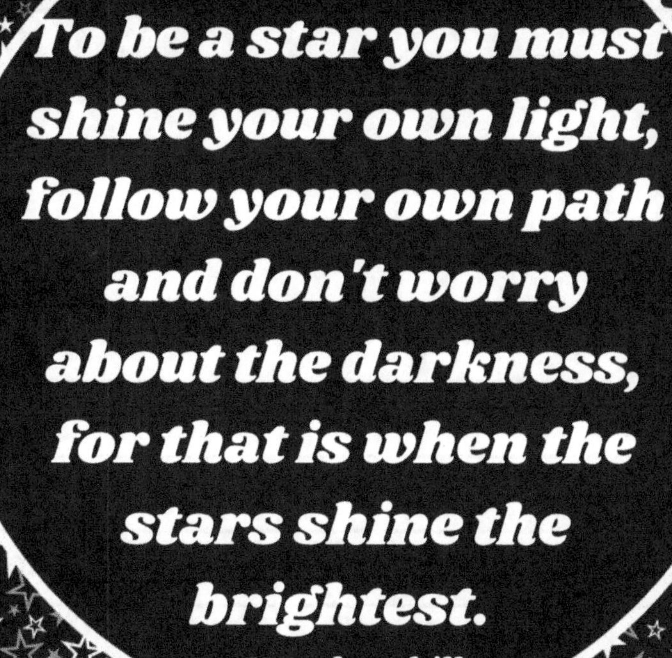

To be a star you must
shine your own light,
follow your own path
and don't worry
about the darkness,
for that is when the
stars shine the
brightest.
~Napoleon hill

Personal Mission Statement:

Craft a statement that defines your purpose as a single mom. How can this mission guide your decisions and actions moving forward?

____

____

____

____

____

____

____

____

____

____

____

____

I will practice
positivity and
patience.

Written in the Stars

Written in the Stars

PRACTICE
YOUR
GRATITUDE

WHAT AM I GRATEFUL FOR?

Black Holes

Dear Single Moms

Beware of Black Holes! This is a reminder to be cautious of anything that fails to enrich your life. Just as stars shine brightly, you deserve relationships and experiences that bring joy, fulfillment, and growth.

In the vast expanse of space, black holes exist as gravitational forces that devour everything around them. Similarly, there may be elements in your life that drain your energy, hinder your progress, and prevent you from reaching your true potential. It's time to take charge, my dear stars, and reclaim control over your journey.

First and foremost, be mindful of dead-end relationships and connections. It could be a lover, a friend, a relative, and even a job. If a connection no longer nurtures your well-being or brings you happiness, it may be time to let go. Surround yourself with individuals who uplift and support you, those who encourage your dreams and aspirations. Cultivate relationships that ignite your inner light and inspire you to grow.
Dear single moms, you are remarkable stars shining in the vastness of the universe. It is within your power to create a life that enriches and empowers you. Reflect on the elements in your life that may be holding you back and take proactive steps to transform them into sources of strength and inspiration.,

Beware of the metaphorical black holes that drain your energy and hinder your growth. Embrace the radiance within you, and let it guide your decisions and actions. Surround yourself with positivity, seek opportunities for growth, and remember that you are deserving of love, success, and happiness.

With warm regards and endless support,

Rikki

Star Advice

Prioritize your mental well-being
and manage stress effectively

- Assess your mental health: Reflect on your stress levels, emotional state, and any signs of burnout.
- Practice self-care: Incorporate activities that promote relaxation, self-reflection, and stress reduction into your routine.
- Seek professional help if needed: Consider therapy or counseling to address mental health concerns or past traumas.
- Build a support system: Surround yourself with understanding friends, family, or support groups.

MENTAL HEALTH

01

02

03

04

05

06

07

08

09

10

START
DATE

END
DATE

Be patient
with me.
I am learning
how to be
happy again.

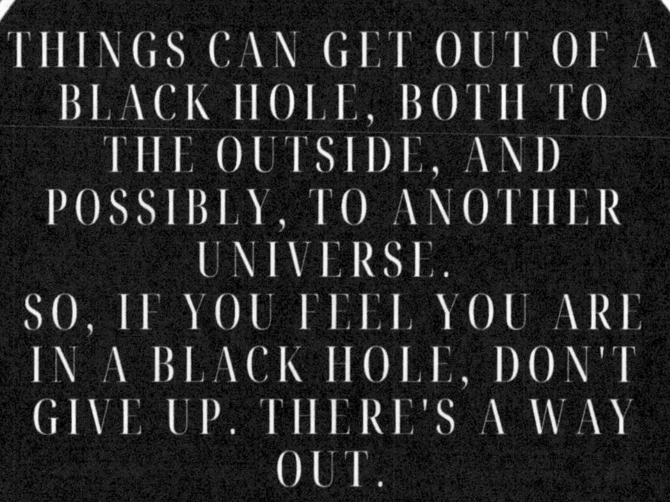

THINGS CAN GET OUT OF A
BLACK HOLE, BOTH TO
THE OUTSIDE, AND
POSSIBLY, TO ANOTHER
UNIVERSE.
SO, IF YOU FEEL YOU ARE
IN A BLACK HOLE, DON'T
GIVE UP. THERE'S A WAY
OUT.

~STEPHEN HAWKING

Beyond Comfort Zones:

Write about a fear you've been avoiding. What steps can you take to face this fear and experience personal growth?

____

____

____

____

____

____

____

____

____

____

____

____

____

Dear Single Mom

I want you to know that as I write this letter, my heart is filled with deep empathy and care for you. I understand the challenges you face as a single mother, as I too have experienced the hardships and trials that come with this journey. I have walked a path marred by domestic violence and endured a harrowing divorce, all while fiercely protecting and caring for my own child. Your struggles are not lost on me, and I want you to know that you are not alone.

First and foremost, I want to emphasize that your safety is of the utmost importance. If you find yourself in an unsafe or abusive relationship, please remember that there is help available to you. I urge you to reach out to organizations and resources that specialize in supporting individuals in such situations. They can provide you with the guidance, protection, and support you need to break free from the cycle of abuse and create a safer environment for yourself and your child.

Here are a few resources that may be able to assist you:
1. National Domestic Violence Hotline: Call 1-800-799-SAFE (7233) or visit www.thehotline.org for immediate help, support, and guidance.
2. Local Women's Shelters: Seek out shelters in your area that provide emergency housing and support services for individuals fleeing domestic violence. They can offer you a safe place to stay and access to vital resources.
3. Legal Aid Organizations: Connect with legal aid organizations that offer free or low-cost legal assistance for survivors of domestic violence. They can help you navigate the legal process, obtain restraining orders, and secure custody arrangements.

Remember, dear single mom, it takes immense strength to recognize when a situation is unsafe and to take the steps necessary to protect yourself and your child. You deserve to live a life free from fear, violence, and oppression. Reach out to these resources, lean on the support they can provide, and know that there is hope for a brighter future.
As you embark on this journaling journey, I hope it serves as a source of solace and empowerment for you. Take this time to prioritize your own healing, growth, and self-care. Reflect on your strengths, set goals for yourself and your child, and envision the life you desire. You have the power within you to create a better future, and I believe in your resilience and determination.

Please know that I am here for you, standing beside you in spirit as you navigate the challenges that come your way. Together, we can create a community of support, understanding, and encouragement for single mothers like ourselves.
Sending you love, strength, and unwavering support.

Rikki

I have the power
to change things
that make me
unhappy.

Self-care is how you take your power back.

~Lalah Delia

Finding Joy:

Describe a simple activity that always brings you joy. How can you incorporate more of these moments into your daily life?

____

I am ready to
work through
my hurt.

STAR BREATHING

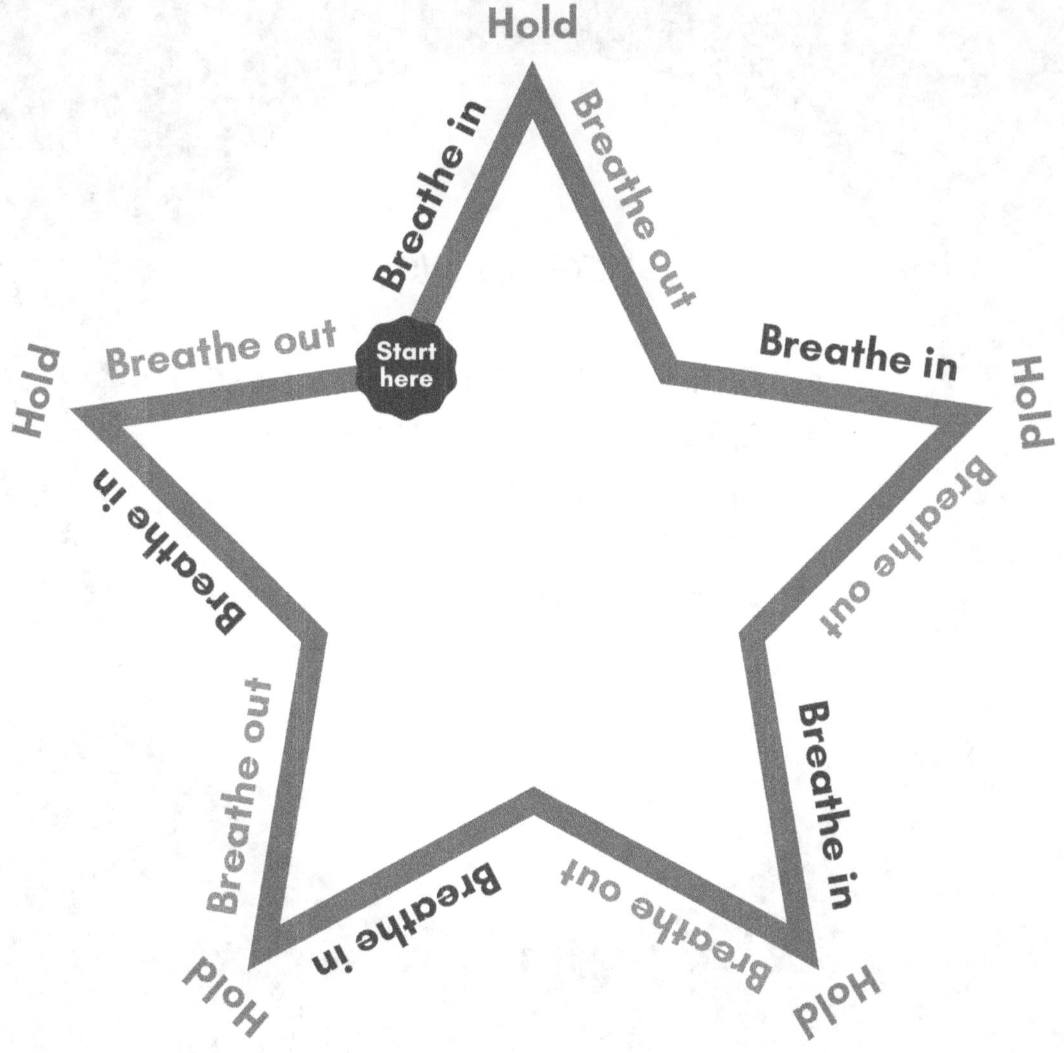

Trace your finger up one side of the star, while you take a deep breath in. Hold your breath at the point and breathe out as you slide down the other side. Keep going until you've gone around the whole star.

Written in the Stars

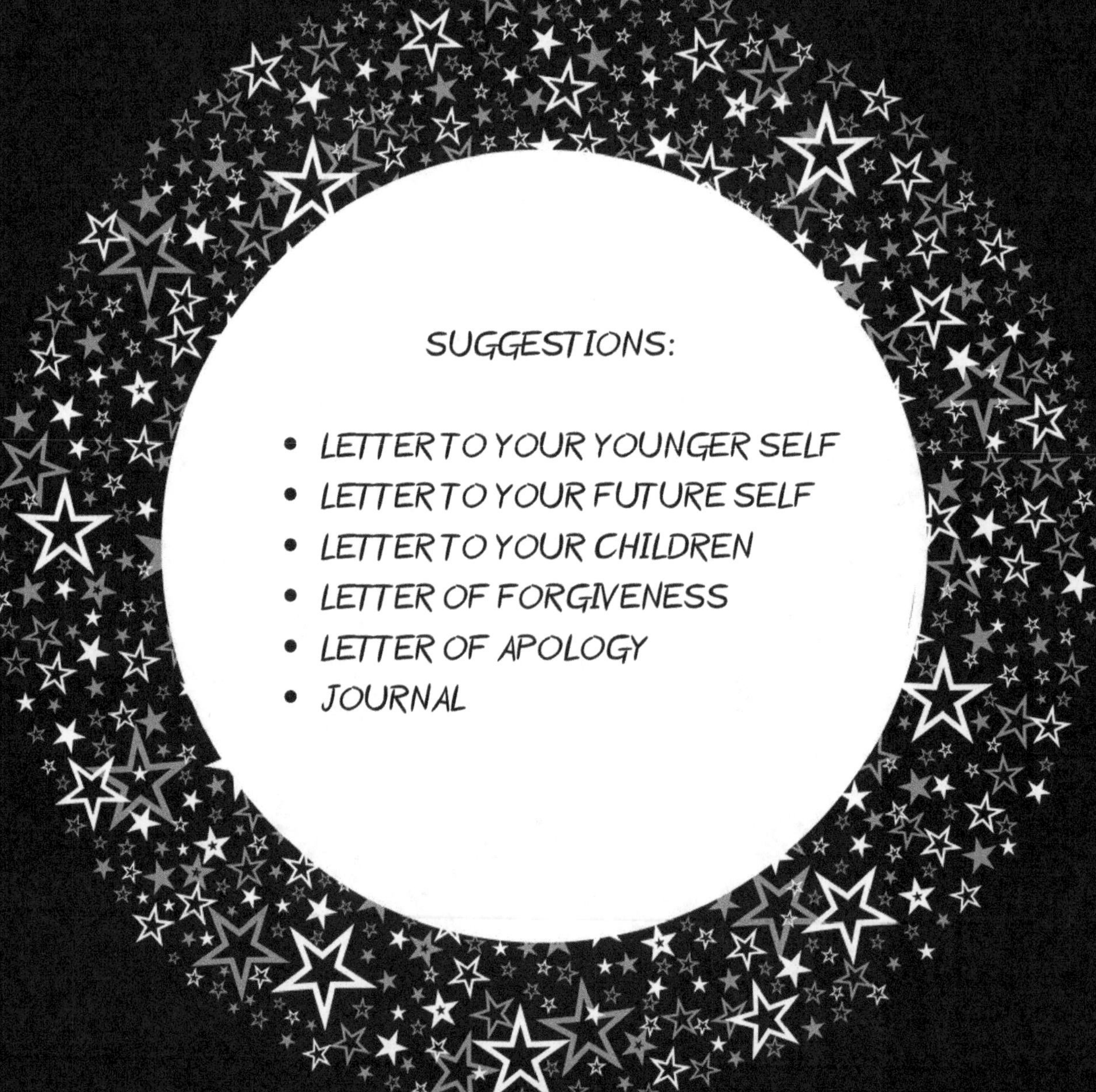

Written in the Stars

Navigating Self-Care:

Detail your ideal self-care routine. How can you prioritize these nurturing practices to maintain balance and well-being?

RELAX

PRACTICE
YOUR
GRATITUDE

WHAT AM I GRATEFUL FOR?

Health

Prioritize your physical well-being and
maintain a healthy lifestyle.
Your health directly impacts your energy levels,
ability to care for your children,
and overall quality of life.

- Evaluate your current health status: Reflect on your eating habits, exercise routine, and overall physical well-being.
- Make healthy food choices: Incorporate nutritious meals and snacks into your daily diet.
- Engage in regular exercise: Find activities that you enjoy and fit them into your schedule, even if it's just short bursts of physical activity.
- Schedule regular check-ups: Ensure you are up to date with medical appointments and screenings.
- Remember, you are capable of taking charge of your health and well-being. Small, consistent steps can make a significant difference in your physical health, allowing you to lead a more vibrant and fulfilling life. Celebrate your progress and be gentle with yourself as you navigate any obstacles that may arise. You deserve a healthy and thriving life, and by prioritizing your health, you are setting an inspiring example for your children. Keep going, and embrace the journey toward a healthier you!

HEALTH

01 ______________________________

02 ______________________________

03 ______________________________

04 ______________________________

05 ______________________________

06 ______________________________

07 ______________________________

08 ______________________________

09 ______________________________

10 ______________________________

START
DATE

END
DATE

Sparkle
and
Shine

Body Positivity:

Reflect on how you perceive your body. How can practicing self-love and embracing your body contribute to your overall self-esteem?

____

____

____

____

____

____

____

____

____

____

____

____

____

I am committed to
being the best
version of myself
that I can be.

Written in the Stars

Written in the Stars

PRACTICE
YOUR
GRATITUDE

WHAT AM I GRATEFUL FOR?

Kids

Twinkle, Twinkle, Little Star

As you embark on the beautiful journey of raising your little ones, I wanted to share some twinkling tips to help you nurture happy, healthy, and well-adjusted children.

1. Nurture Connection: Foster a deep emotional bond with your children. Spend quality time together, engage in meaningful conversations, and create traditions that build strong connections. Be present and listen attentively to their thoughts and feelings, allowing them to feel valued and heard.
2. Establish Routine and Stability: Children thrive on routine and stability. Create a consistent daily routine that includes regular mealtimes, sleep schedules, and designated study or playtime. Consistency provides a sense of security and helps children develop healthy habits.
3. Encourage Independence: Support your children's independence by allowing them age-appropriate responsibilities. Encourage them to make choices, solve problems, and take on tasks that build confidence and resilience. Celebrate their accomplishments and provide gentle guidance when needed.
4. Foster a Positive Environment: Create a home filled with love, positivity, and respect. Model kindness, empathy, and good behavior. Teach your children the importance of gratitude, forgiveness, and embracing diversity. Encourage open communication and create space for them to express their thoughts and emotions.
5. Seek parenting resources: Research books, articles, or classes on child development and effective parenting techniques.
6. Seek Support: Remember that it's okay to ask for help. Reach out to friends, family, or support groups that can offer guidance, a helping hand, or simply a listening ear. Building a network of support will provide you and your children with a strong foundation.
7. I want to remind you of the utmost importance of your own well-being. You are the guiding star in your children's lives, and they look to you for love, guidance, and stability. For them to truly thrive, they need to see you thrive as well. When you prioritize your well-being, you teach them the importance of self-care, resilience, and setting boundaries. You show them that they too can pursue their dreams and reach for the stars. Each decision you make, each step you take, shapes the trajectory of your journey and the lives of your children.

Co-Parenting as a Single Mom

My dear friend. As stars shine together in the night sky, your journey as a single mom can be made brighter by embracing the art of co-parenting. I wanted to offer you some friendly advice on how to navigate this path with grace and strength.

Communication is Key: Open and honest communication with your co-parent is vital. Keep the lines of communication open, sharing updates about your children's well-being, milestones, and challenges. Respectful and effective communication will foster a healthy co-parenting relationship.

Focus on the Children: Remember that your children's needs come first. Prioritize their well-being and ensure they feel loved and supported by both parents. Create a consistent and harmonious environment by aligning on rules, routines, and discipline strategies.

Embrace Flexibility: Co-parenting requires flexibility and compromise. Be open to adjusting schedules and making compromises for the sake of your children's happiness and stability. Demonstrating flexibility will also encourage the same behavior from your co-parent.

Nurture a Positive Environment: Encourage positivity and avoid negative talk or conflicts in front of your children. Create a peaceful and supportive atmosphere where your children can thrive. Celebrate each other's successes and support one another in your parenting roles.

Seek Support: Surround yourself with a support network of friends, family, or support groups who understand the unique challenges of single parenting. Lean on them for guidance, advice, and a listening ear during difficult times.

Remember, dear friend, that you are not alone in this journey. Just as stars guide sailors at sea, your love and dedication will guide your children through life's ups and downs. Embrace co-parenting with patience, understanding, and a shared commitment to your children's happiness.

Wishing you a co-parenting journey filled with harmony and love,

Rikki

KIDS

01

02

03

04

05

06

07

08

09

10

START
DATE

END
DATE

UP ABOVE THE WORLD SO HIGH, LIKE A DIAMOND IN THE SKY

I choose peace.

Relationship Harmony:

Reflect on your communication with your children. How can you enhance your connection by actively listening and fostering open dialogue?

____

____

____

____

____

____

____

____

____

____

____

____

CONNECTIONS

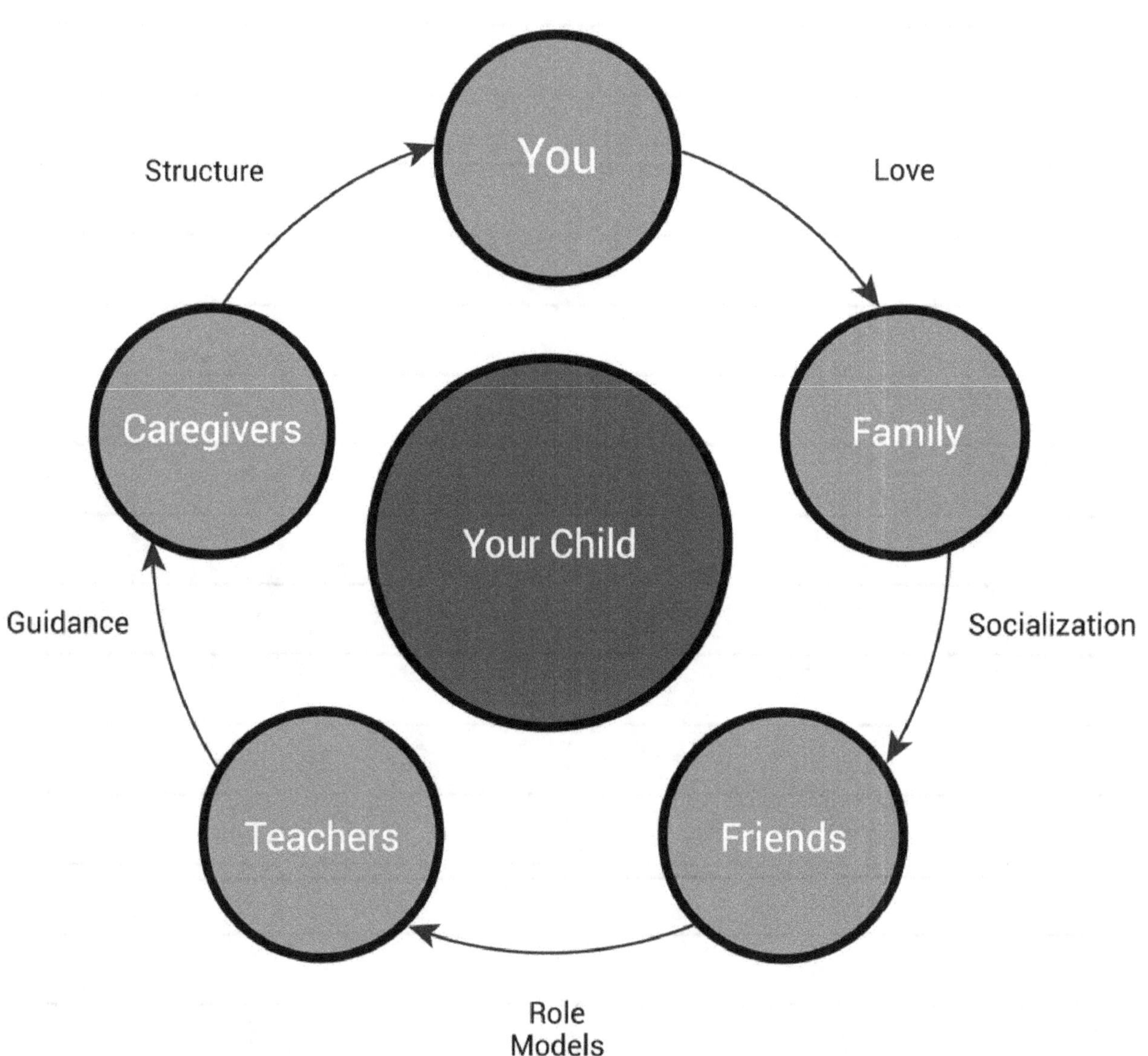

MESSAGE

In the middle of the circle is your child- the center of your universe. In order to surround them with the essentials that they need to thrive, it is crucial that we develop connections.

You are the guiding star of someone's existence.

~Carroll Bryant

Embracing Imperfections:

Describe a parenting moment when you felt less than perfect. How can you show yourself compassion and acknowledge that imperfections are a part of growth?

____
____
____
____
____
____
____
____
____
____
____
____
____

I am a
great mom!

Dream
Big

Legacy Reflection:

Imagine your children reflecting on your journey years from now. What values and lessons do you hope they take with them as they navigate their own paths?

____

____

____

____

____

____

____

____

____

____

____

____

____

Written in the Stars

SUGGESTIONS:

- LETTER TO YOUR YOUNGER SELF
- LETTER TO YOUR FUTURE SELF
- LETTER TO YOUR CHILDREN
- LETTER OF FORGIVENESS
- LETTER OF APOLOGY
- JOURNAL

Written in the Stars

Parenting Values:

Define three core values you want to instill in your children. How can you model these values in your own actions and decisions?

____

____

____

____

____

____

____

____

____

____

____

____

____

"While you might be doubting yourself, someone is admiring your strength"

PRACTICE
YOUR
GRATITUDE

WHAT AM I GRATEFUL FOR?

Support

Constellations

Dear Single Moms

In the vast expanse of the night sky, among the celestial wonders, there exists a constellation known as Cassiopeia. It consists of only five bright stars, arranged in a distinctive shape that has captivated stargazers for centuries. Today, I want to share with you the parallel between Cassiopeia and the importance of seeking out genuine support in your journey as single moms.

Just like the stars that form Cassiopeia, true support can be found in the quality of connections, rather than the quantity. In this fast-paced world, it's easy to get caught up in the illusion of having numerous friends or acquaintances. But, dear single moms, remember that one truly good friend holds more power and support than a thousand superficial connections.

In the sky, Cassiopeia shines brightly, standing out among the countless stars. Similarly, a genuine friend stands by your side, providing unwavering support and understanding. This friend listens to your joys and triumphs, as well as your fears and struggles, without judgment or ulterior motives. They celebrate your victories and offer comfort during challenging times.

Just as Cassiopeia's stars remain constant, a true friend remains steadfast, a beacon of light in your life. They lend a helping hand, offering practical assistance or simply being there to lend an ear when you need someone to talk to. They understand the importance of your well-being and encourage you to prioritize self-care. With their presence, you never feel alone, for they remind you that you are valued and loved.

Contrastingly, a multitude of acquaintances may flicker in and out of your life like passing meteors. They may offer temporary distractions or superficial interactions, but when the storm clouds gather, they may fade away, leaving you feeling isolated and unsupported. Quantity may seem impressive, but it is the quality of friendships that sustains us through the darkest nights.

So, dear single moms, I urge you to seek out those true stars, those friends who genuinely care about your well-being and your children's happiness. Nurture those connections that bring positivity, support, and encouragement into your life. Surround yourself with friends who uplift and inspire, who offer a helping hand without expecting anything in return.

Remember, you deserve genuine friendships that add light and joy to your journey. Just as Cassiopeia's stars illuminate the night sky, these friendships will illuminate your path, guiding you through the challenges of single motherhood. Together, you can create constellations of love, strength, and support.

If you have yet to find that one special friend, fear not. Reach out to support networks, community groups, or counseling services that can connect you with like-minded individuals who understand your journey. Be open to forming new bonds, and trust that the universe will bring those kindred spirits into your life.

Single moms, like stars, possess extraordinary strength and resilience. Embrace the power of genuine connections, for they will serve as your guiding stars on this beautiful journey. Trust in the constellations of friendship that will provide you and your children with the love and support you truly deserve.

May the light of Cassiopeia remind you of the importance of seeking true friendships, and may these connections bring you boundless love and strength.

With heartfelt support,

Rikki

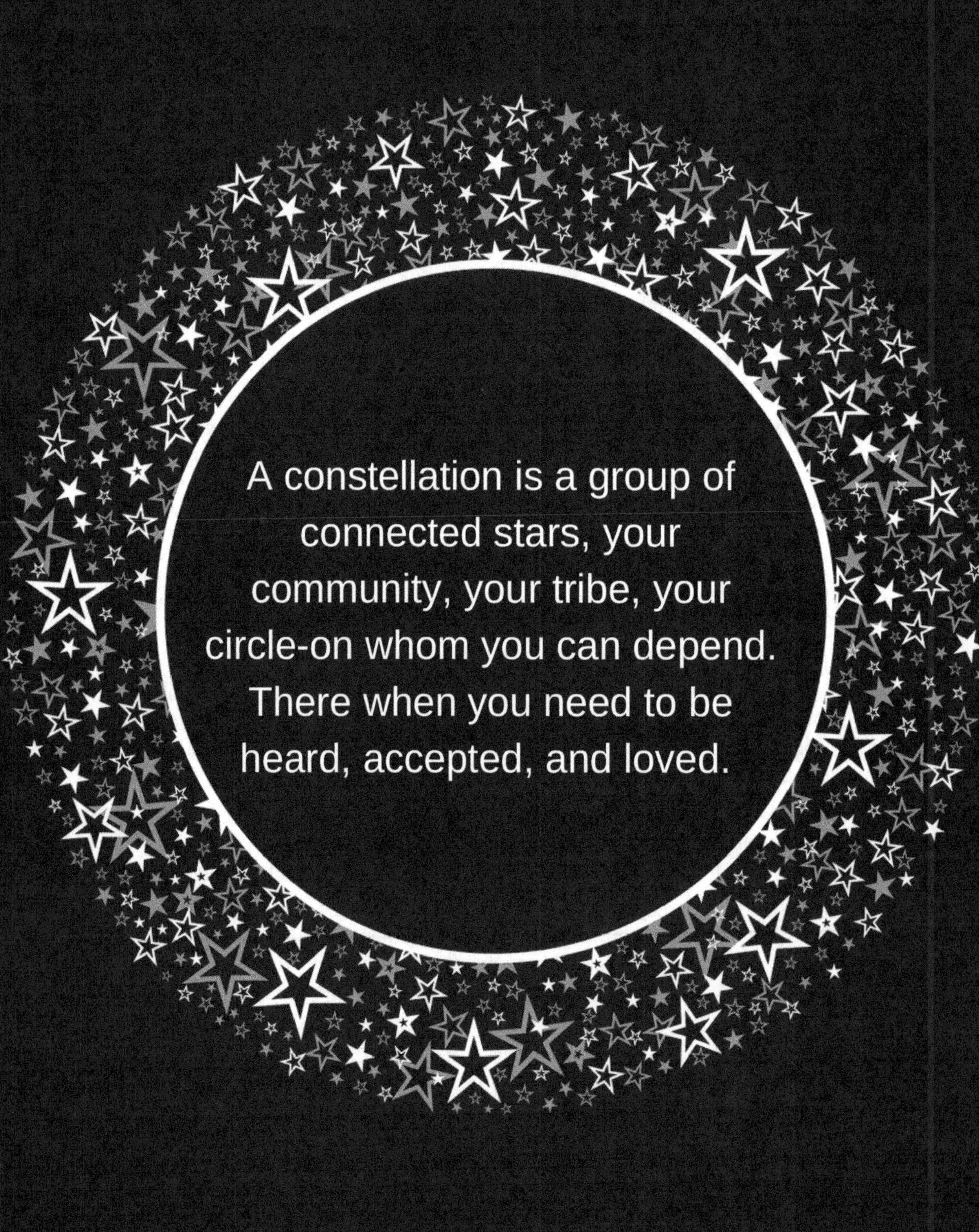
A constellation is a group of
connected stars, your
community, your tribe, your
circle-on whom you can depend.
There when you need to be
heard, accepted, and loved.

Star Advice

Build and maintain a strong social support
network that provides emotional support,
reduces isolation, and offers
practical assistance when needed.

- Identify supportive individuals: Reflect on your existing relationships and identify people who offer support and positivity.
- Cultivate new connections: Seek out like-minded individuals through social activities, support groups, or online communities.
- Reach out for help: Don't hesitate to ask for assistance from friends, family, or support organizations when needed.
- Be proactive: Offer support and reciprocate the help you receive, nurturing mutually beneficial relationships.

SUPPORT

01

02

03

04

05

06

07

08

09

10

START
DATE

END
DATE

Ask the universe to help you meet your soul tribe. Find your people so that you have the support and love you deserve. Connect and grow with other awakened souls.

Guiding Star

Dear Single Mothers

In the vastness of the night sky, amidst the twinkling stars that adorn the darkness, there is always one star that stands out—the guiding star. It shines with a brilliance that captivates, guiding wanderers and sailors alike on their journeys. Today, I want to remind you, dear single mothers, of the importance of seeking a guiding light for your mental well-being—a mentor, therapist, or faith leader who can offer support and guidance in your beautiful yet challenging path.

Just as stars navigate the celestial expanse, illuminating the way for lost travelers, a guiding light can help navigate the complexities of life, offering clarity, strength, and understanding. As a single mother, you face unique challenges, juggling multiple roles and responsibilities. It is essential to recognize the significance of nurturing your own mental well-being, for it is through self-care that you can truly thrive and provide the best for your children.

Consider seeking a mentor who has walked a similar path, someone who can share wisdom gained through experience. A mentor can offer guidance, support, and practical advice, helping you navigate the intricacies of single motherhood. They can provide a listening ear, a shoulder to lean on, and insights that empower you to make informed decisions for yourself and your children.

Alternatively, a therapist can be your guiding star in times of emotional turbulence. Just as stars illuminate the night, therapists provide a safe space where you can explore your thoughts, emotions, and experiences. They can help you navigate the challenges of parenting, unravel any unresolved issues, and equip you with coping mechanisms to manage stress, anxiety, or depression. A therapist can serve as a beacon of hope, reminding you that seeking support is not a sign of weakness but a courageous step towards self-growth.

For those who find solace in faith, a faith leader can be a guiding light on your spiritual journey. They can provide guidance, offer words of encouragement, and help you find meaning and purpose in your experiences. Faith leaders can lend a listening ear, help you deepen your connection to your spirituality, and provide a sense of community and belonging that nurtures your soul.

Remember, dear single mothers, you do not have to face the challenges alone. Seeking a guiding light does not diminish your strength; rather, it amplifies it. It takes courage to acknowledge that you deserve support and to actively seek it. Just as stars shine brightest in constellations, your light shines brightest when nurtured by the support and guidance of others.

As you embark on this journey of self-discovery and growth, trust that there are guiding lights out there who are ready to walk alongside you. Reach out, connect, and allow yourself to be supported. Embrace the opportunity to grow, learn, and thrive as you create a brighter future for yourself and your children.

The night sky is vast and filled with countless stars, each with its own story and purpose. Similarly, your journey as a single mother is unique and holds immense potential. Seek your guiding star, embrace the support of a mentor, therapist, or faith leader, and let their light guide you towards the path of self-care, healing, and personal growth.

May your guiding light bring you clarity, resilience, and renewed hope as you navigate the vastness of single motherhood.

With heartfelt encouragement,

Rikki

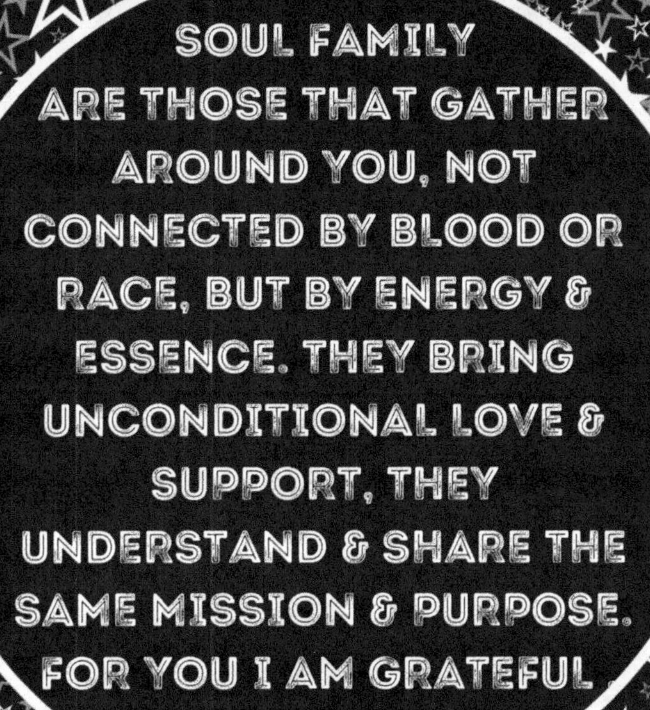
SOUL FAMILY
ARE THOSE THAT GATHER
AROUND YOU, NOT
CONNECTED BY BLOOD OR
RACE, BUT BY ENERGY &
ESSENCE. THEY BRING
UNCONDITIONAL LOVE &
SUPPORT, THEY
UNDERSTAND & SHARE THE
SAME MISSION & PURPOSE.
FOR YOU I AM GRATEFUL

I am thankful for
those who provide
us with love and
support.

Forging Connections:

Describe a moment when you felt a strong sense of community and connection. How can you foster and contribute to these meaningful connections?

____

____

____

____

____

____

____

____

____

____

____

____

Written in the Stars

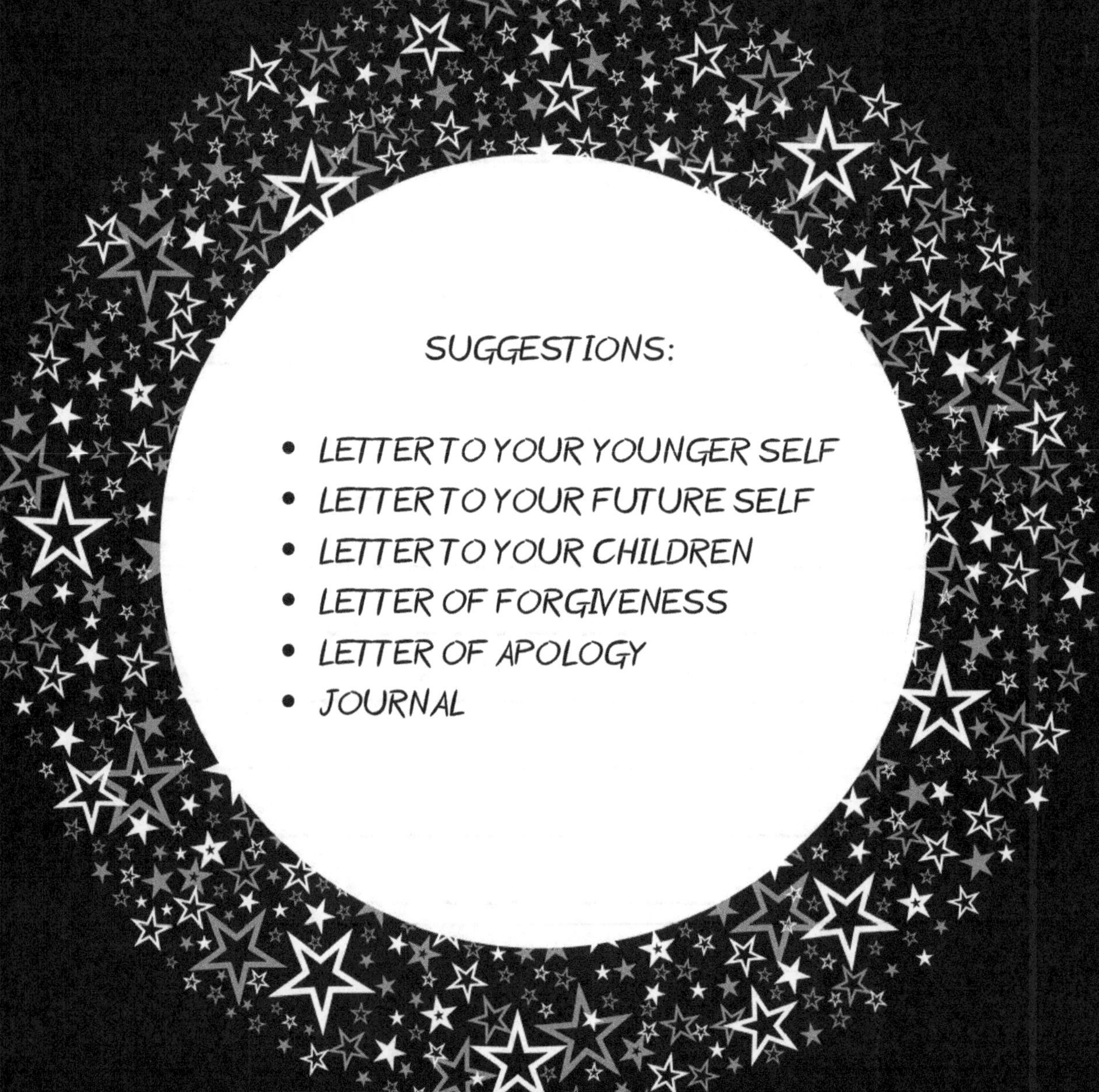

Written in the Stars

Kindness Ripple:

Describe an act of kindness you've extended or received. How can nurturing this kindness create a positive ripple effect in your life?

Defining Boundaries:

Identify an area where you need to establish clearer boundaries. How can setting these boundaries improve your relationships and well-being?

Mentorship Reflection:

Write about someone who has served as a positive mentor or role model in your life. How can you integrate their wisdom into your journey?

____

____

____

____

____

____

____

____

____

____

____

____

____

____

PRACTICE
YOUR
GRATITUDE

WHAT AM I GRATEFUL FOR?

DON'T WAIT
FOR THE STARS
TO ALIGN.
REACH UP AND
ARRANGE THEM
THE WAY YOU
WANT.
~PHARRELL WILLIAMS

I welcome
happiness and
abundance
into my life.

Outro

Dear Star,

As I reach the closing chapter, I hope you've found this book to be an uplifting beacon of hope! I want to take a moment to celebrate you. You are a shining star, illuminating the path of personal growth and empowerment for yourself and your little ones. Throughout this journal, you have demonstrated unwavering commitment and dedication to your journey, and I am in awe of your strength and resilience.

I am truly grateful for the opportunity to connect with you and guide you along this transformative path. Thank you for allowing me on the journey with you as you delved deep within yourself, exploring your dreams, fears, and aspirations. Your willingness to embark on this journey of self-discovery is a testament to your courage and determination.

Remember, dear star, you are never alone. In the Resources section at the end of this journal, you will discover a constellation of helpful websites tailored for single moms, providing you with further support on your journey. There are also websites, blogs, Facebook groups, and Instagram pages filled with stories of other single mom stars who are walking a similar path. Reach out to them, connect with them, and together, you can create a powerful network of support and understanding. Share your experiences, offer encouragement, and celebrate each other's triumphs along the way.

I want you to know that your light shines brightly, and you have the power to create a beautiful and fulfilling life for yourself and your little ones. Even on the darkest nights, remember that you possess an inner radiance that can guide you through any challenge. Trust in your abilities, believe in your dreams, and know that you have the strength within you to overcome any obstacle.

May your journey continue to be filled with love, joy, and abundance. Keep shining brightly, dear star, and know that you have the power to create the life you desire. With heartfelt gratitude and endless encouragement,

Rikki

Joyful Traditions:

Describe a meaningful family tradition you want to establish. How can these traditions strengthen your family's bond and create lasting memories?

____

____

____

____

____

____

____

____

____

____

____

____

____

____

____

STAR

You've made it this far and I think that's really BRAVE!

Mindful Presence:

Detail a moment when you felt fully present with your child. How does being mindful enhance the quality of your interactions?

____

____

____

____

____

____

____

____

____

____

____

____

FIND YOUR TRIBE.

YOU KNOW, THE ONES THAT MAKE YOU
FEEL THE MOST YOU. THE ONES THAT
LIFT YOU UP AND HELP YOU REMEMBER
WHO YOU REALLY ARE. THE ONES THAT
REMIND YOU THAT A BLIP IN THE ROAD
IS JUST THAT, A BLIP. THEY ARE THE ONES
THAT, WHEN YOU WALK OUT OF A ROOM,
THEY MAKE YOU FEEL LIKE A BETTER
PERSON THAN WHEN YOU WALKED IN.
THEY ARE THE ONES THAT, EVEN IF YOU
DON'T SEE THEM FACE TO FACE AS OFTEN
AS YOU'D LIKE, YOU SEE THEM HEART TO
HEART. YOU KNOW THAT KIND OF TRIBE?
WHO'S YOUR TRIBE?

– JENNIFER PASTILOFF

I am grateful
for motherhood.

Empowering Affirmations:

Create a list of positive affirmations that reflect your personal strengths. How can incorporating these affirmations into your routine boost your self-esteem?

____

____

____

____

____

____

____

____

____

____

____

____

____

Written in the Stars

SUGGESTIONS:

- LETTER TO YOUR YOUNGER SELF
- LETTER TO YOUR FUTURE SELF
- LETTER TO YOUR CHILDREN
- LETTER OF FORGIVENESS
- LETTER OF APOLOGY
- JOURNAL

Written in the Stars

Unveiling Passions:

Reflect on a hobby or interest you've set aside. How can rediscovering this passion contribute to your sense of fulfillment?

____
____
____
____
____
____
____
____
____
____
____
____
____

Fearless Dreams:

Envision your boldest dream, regardless of any limitations. What steps can you take to move closer to turning this dream into reality?

PRACTICE
YOUR
GRATITUDE

WHAT AM I GRATEFUL FOR?

Sunday Self-Care Bingo

MEDITATE	LISTEN TO MUSIC	CATCH UP WITH FRIENDS	GO FOR A WALK	SMILE
TRY A NEW RECIPE	PLAY A GAME	READ A BOOK	GO TO THE PARK	COFFEE WITH A FRIEND
GET A MANI-PEDI	DRINK WATER	★	TAKE A SOCIAL MEDIA BREAK	TAKE A LONG BATH
DANCE	8 HOURS OF SLEEP	BUY A PLANT	HUG MY CHILDREN	DROP A HABIT THAT IS NOT FOR ME
GET OUT IN NATURE	30 MINUTES OF EXERCISE	DECLUTTER MY SPACE	WRITE A POEM	JOURNAL

Wellness Wheel

THE WELLNESS WHEEL IS A GREAT TOOL THAT HELPS
YOU BETTER UNDERSTAND WHAT YOU CAN DO TO
MAKE YOUR LIFE MORE BALANCED. THINK ABOUT
THE 8 LIFE CATEGORIES BELOW, AND RATE THEM
FROM 1 - 10.

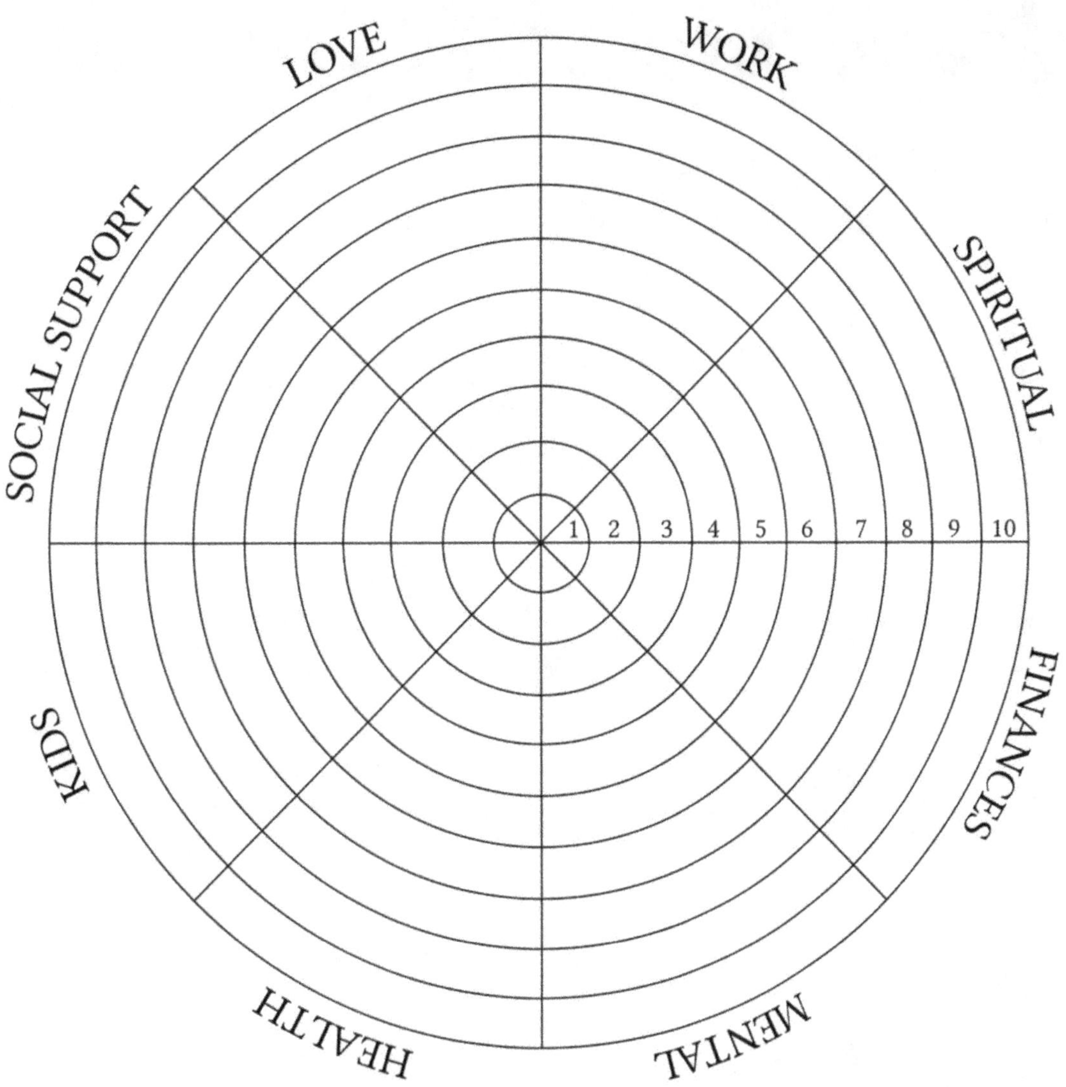

Love (Red), Work (Orange), Spiritual (Yellow), Finances (Green), Mental (BLUE), Health (Purple), Kids (Aqua),
Social Support (Pink)

Resources

FINANCIAL PLANNING RESOURCES
GreenPath Financial Wellness
https://www.greenpath.com/
Financial Counseling Services
GreenPath Financial Wellness is a trusted national nonprofit with more than 60-years of helping people build financial health and resiliency. Our NFCC-certified counselors give you options to manage credit card debt, student loans and homeownership.
Take Advantage of GreenPath's Free Online Financial Education. Explore GreenPath's LearningLab for all things financial. We bring you well researched courses and tools to enable a better understanding of money for a healthy financial life.
https://www.greenpath.com/learninglab/
Consumer Financial Protection Bureau
https://www.consumerfinance.gov/consumer-tools/
Consumer resources: Wherever you are on your financial journey, you can prepare yourself to make informed financial decisions with these resources.
National Foundation for Credit Counseling (NFCC)
https://www.nfcc.org/how-we-help/
As one of the oldest networks of nonprofit financial counseling agencies, the NFCC is here to help you defeat your debt and look forward with confidence. While financial situations may differ from person to person, debt can feel overwhelming no matter the amount. In just one session, typically 30 minutes to an hour, an NFCC Certified Counselor will speak with you about your current financial circumstances and help create an actionable plan to tackle your debt. No loans. No hidden fees. No hassle.
Foundation for Financial Planning: Navigating Your Financial Roadmap Workbook (PDF)
https://ffpprobono.org/.../Navigating-Your-Financial...

Star Support

FDIC

How Money Smart Are You? is our new suite of 14 financial games and related resources. It's available in both English and Spanish.

Earn (virtual) coins, have some fun, and learn about everyday financial topics.

You can play with or without an account – it's your choice and explained on the site. If you want an account, create one on the site. Accounts from the Money Smart Computer-Based Instruction (CBI) product will not transfer to How Money Smart Are You?

MyMoney .gov

https://www.mymoney.gov/tools

This page can help you locate and use on-line calculators, budget worksheets, planning checklists and other helpful resources from the federal government for making financial decisions.

National Endowment for Financial Education (NEFE)

https://www.nefe.org/.../Your-Spending-Your-Savings-Your...

Your Spending, Your Saving, Your Future

This all-in-one guide addresses financial goal-setting, getting out of debt, using bank accounts and credit card, monitoring and controlling spending, and boosting savings and investments.

Money Sense Complete Financial Plan Toolkit

https://www.moneysense.ca/.../the-moneysense-complete.../

10 worksheets that will allow you to prepare your own professional-quality personal financial plan. You can download each one as a PDF to print out and fill in with pencil or pen, or you can download them as Microsoft Word files, and fill them in on your computer.

Mapping Your Future: Budget Calculator

http://mappingyourfuture.org/money/budgetcalculator.cfm

Manage Your Debt

Being in debt can be an overwhelming and debilitating experience. But there are smart, proven ways to manage your debt and bring you back into sound financial health. Take the time to examine all your options and pick ones that will help you the most.

https://www.debt.org/manage/...

Star Support

Benefit Finder
Benefits.gov is an online resource to help you find federal benefits you may be eligible for in the United States.
https://www.benefits.gov/
SmartCredit
Get on top of your Credit Scores and Reports & take action directly with your creditors through our patented online system.
https://www.smartcredit.com/
WIFE.org
The Women's Institute for Financial Education (WIFE.org) is the oldest non-profit organization dedicated to providing financial education to women in their quest for financial independence.
https://www.wife.org/
Collection Shield 360
Collection Shield 360 utilizes it's experience and knowledge of these laws to prepare and send credit repair disputes on your behalf, to help you remove inaccurate or unverifiable collection accounts from your credit reports.
https://www.collectionshield360.com/
Understanding Retirement Plan Options
https://www.360financialliteracy.org/.../Understanding...
What is a Credit Score
https://www.consumerfinance.gov/.../what-is-a-credit.../
Free Credit Coaching
A debt relief organization providing free financial counseling and education. We will discuss the options of affordable Debt Management Programs to those ready to take control of their financial well-being.
https://credit.org/
Energy Saving Tips for Renters
https://www.energystar.gov/products/top_10_tips_renters
Debt Relief vs Bankruptcy: Which is Right for You?
https://www.incharge.org/.../debt-settlement-vs.../

Star Support

NFCC

https://www.nfcc.org/

Our programs and services are accessed through our national network of nonprofit member agencies. Each agency is staffed by NFCC Certified Financial Counselors. These individuals are financial advocates who can help you get started with a financial review and establish a budget and a personalized financial action plan.

Wealthy Single Mommy

https://www.wealthysinglemommy.com/category/career/

Single moms, and women thinking about being single moms, have certain responsibilities, challenges, fears and joys when it comes to money.

The Budget Mom

https://www.thebudgetmom.com/

Simple, easy-to-follow solutions to help you budget your money, pay off debt, save more, and crush your financial goals. But more than that, I give you the tools to start doing the things that matter most to you, on a budget that actually works!

12 Best Personal Finance Courses

https://money.usnews.com/.../worthwhile-online-personal...

If you never learned how to manage money well, it's not too late to take an online class.

Self

https://www.self.inc/

Build credit while saving money. Self is helping thousands of people begin their financial journey with a Credit Builder Account. We understand that building a financial foundation is a daunting task for most people, so we're dedicated to building a product that will help our customers move two steps in the right direction.

HEALTH & NUTRITION RESOURCES

Commodity Supplemental Food Program (CSFP)

Child and Adult Care Food Program

https://www.fns.usda.gov/cacfp
The Child and Adult Care Food Program (CACFP) is a federal program that provides reimbursements for nutritious meals and snacks to eligible children and adults who are enrolled for care at participating child care centers, day care homes, and adult day care centers. CACFP also provides reimbursements for meals served to children and youth participating in afterschool care programs, children residing in emergency shelters, and adults over the age of 60 or living with a disability and enrolled in day care facilities. CACFP contributes to the wellness, healthy growth, and development of young children and adults in the United States.

The Emergency Food Assistance Program (TEFAP)
https://www.benefits.gov/benefit/681
Helps supplement the diets of low-income Americans, including elderly people, by providing them with emergency food assistance at no cost. Through TEFAP, the U.S. Department of Agriculture (USDA) purchases a variety of nutritious, high-quality USDA Foods and makes them available to state distributing agencies.

Food and Nutrition Services State Directory
https://www.fns.usda.gov/contacts?f%5B0%5D=program%3A27

Supplemental Nutrition Assistance Program (SNAP)
https://www.fns.usda.gov/snap/recipient/eligibility
SNAP provides nutrition benefits to supplement the food budget of needy families so they can purchase healthy food and move towards self-sufficiency.

Food Pantry Directory
https://www.foodpantries.org/ Free food pantries are located near you, me, and most families, no matter where they live. There are tens of thousands of charities, churches, non-profits, and other groups that work to feed struggling households. Even if a food bank is not near where you may live, they may still offer referrals or even a low cost delivery service.

United Way 211
Dial 211 or visit https://www.211.org/services/essential-needs
Will help you find local resources for food, housing, childcare, and more. Reach out to your pediatrician or local hospital. Pediatricians usually get samples of formula (so do some hospitals), so reach out. If you're eligible for WIC or SNAP benefits, both may have infant formula as well. Other places to check: Women's shelters, food banks, and faith-based organizations that provide food assistance.

Special Supplemental Nutrition Assistance Program for Women, Infants and Children (WIC)

https://www.fns.usda.gov/wic

Provides federal grants to states for supplemental foods, health care referrals, and nutrition education for low-income pregnant, breastfeeding, and non-breastfeeding postpartum women, and to infants and children up to age five who are found to be at nutritional risk.

WIC Farmers' Market Nutrition Program (FMNP)

https://www.fns.usda.gov/.../wic-farmers-market-nutrition...

Eligible WIC participants are issues FMNP coupons in addition to their regular WIC benefits. These coupons can be used to buy eligible foods from farmers, farmers markets, or roadside stands that have been approved by the state agency to accept FMNP coupons.

Community Health Center Locator

https://findahealthcenter.hrsa.gov/

Planned Parenthood - Women's Services

https://www.plannedparenthood.org/.../our.../womens-services

We provide essential reproductive and sexual health services like pelvic exams, Pap tests, cancer screenings, and testing and treatment for vaginal infections.

Planned Parenthood - General Healthcare

https://www.plannedparenthood.org/.../general-health-care

Routine visits with a health care provider are an important part of taking care of our health. Your nurse or doctor can give you important information about your personal health, help you prevent illness, and provide treatments for any problems you may have.

Together RX Access

http://trxaccess.org/

Through this website, we also connect you with information about the Health Insurance Marketplace, the Affordable Care Act, individual pharmaceutical company patient assistance programs, and other patient assistance resources. With Together Rx Access®, uninsured Americans gain access to immediate savings on prescription products at their neighborhood pharmacies AND resources that help people take care of what's most important—their health.

Dental Assistance

https://www.needhelppayingbills.com/html/dental_clinics.html

Many of the patients (adults or children) may not have access to proper care due to lack of a health insurance plan or maybe the coverage on their current insurance policy does not pay for dental care, exams, or cleaning. Other families need help as maybe their household income is too low to pay for any type of medical or dental bills. There are numerous free dental clinics near you listed by state below, government programs, and other resources that people can turn to for assistance.

NURX

https://www.nurx.com/our-method/

We take the stress out of taking care of yourself. Our brand of healthcare is simple, confidential, and seamless.

Lasagna Love

https://lasagnalove.org/

Lasagna Love is a global nonprofit and grassroots movement that aims to positively impact communities by connecting neighbors with neighbors through homemade meal delivery. We also seek to eliminate stigmas associated with asking for help when it is needed most. Our mission is simple: feed families, spread kindness, and strengthen communities.

GoodRx

https://www.goodrx.com/

GoodRx is a free mobile app and website that helps Americans save millions of dollars every month by finding them the lowest prescription prices in their neighborhood.

Medicaid & CHIP

https://www.healthcare.gov/medicaid-chip/

Medicaid and the Children's Health Insurance Program (CHIP) provide free or low-cost health coverage to millions of Americans, including some low-income people, families and children, pregnant women, the elderly, and people with disabilities.

VSP Vision Care

https://www.vsp.com/

Many people go without vision care and struggle to see and feel their best. Sight is our window to wellness, so we're committed to bringing together the best people, products, and services to deliver greater access to high-quality, affordable eye care and eyewear. Because everyone deserves to see well and live happy.

Benefit Finder

https://www.benefits.gov/

Benefits.gov is an online resource to help you find federal benefits you may be eligible for in the United States.

FAMILY LAW RESOURCES

WomensLaw

https://www.womenslaw.org

Despite its name, WomensLaw.org provides information that is relevant to people of all genders, not just women. Our Email Hotline will provide legal information to anyone who reaches out with legal questions or concerns regarding domestic violence, sexual violence, or any other topic covered on WomensLaw.org.

State Child Support Calculators

https://www.alllaw.com/calculators/childsupport

Each state has it's own statutory guidelines that judges use to determine the amount of monthly child support paid by the non-custodial parent. Link provides guidelines for each.

How to Make Your Parenting Plan or Agreement

https://www.custodyxchange.com/.../ove.../parenting-plan.php

Your parenting plan or custody agreement outlines how you and the other parent will continue to care and provide for your children after you separate. An effective plan is personalized to fit the needs of your family situation and contains the following information.

What Happens if the Non-Custodial Parent Misses Visitation?

https://www.divorceandfinance.org/what-happens-if-the.../

Find out what happens if a non-custodial parent misses visitation and other information relevant to this situation such as a general overview of visitation rights, the consequences of missing them, and the process involved in dealing with missed visitations.

Legal Services Corporation

https://www.lsc.gov/

LSC is the single largest funder of civil legal aid for low-income Americans in the nation. Established in 1974, LSC operates as an independent 501(c)(3) nonprofit corporation that promotes equal access to justice and provides grants for high-quality civil legal assistance to low-income Americans. LSC distributes more than 90 percent of its total funding to 132 independent nonprofit legal aid programs with more than 800 offices.

NOLO

Nolo has an extensive library of legal articles—all for free. The law can be hard to find, complex, and intimidating. We strive to make it accessible to everyone—to help people find answers to their everyday legal and business questions.

LawHelp

LawHelp helps people of low and moderate incomes find free legal aid programs in their communities, answers to questions about their legal rights and forms to help them with their legal problems.

Child Custody Mediation: How It Works and Tips for Success
https://www.divorcenet.com/.../understanding-child...
Learn the basics of this dispute resolution tool for divorcing spouses and get pointers on approaching your own child custody mediation sessions.
Contempt of Court for Child Custody
https://www.legalmatch.com/.../contempt-of-court-for...
How to File and Prepare for a Child Custody Case
https://www.divorcenet.com/.../how-to-file-and-prepare...
Learn how child custody cases work, including how to open a case, get help agreeing on a parenting plan, and prepare for a custody hearing.
Documentation in Child Custody Cases
https://alimentor.org/.../documentation-in-child-custody...
Increase your chances of reaching an optimum child custody agreement by collecting and organizing the right evidence.
Guide to Presenting Evidence in Family Court
https://resources.hellodivorce.com/guide-to-presenting...
Why? Well, many judges review the evidence (out-of-court statements, school records, agreements, police reports, financial records, property titles, proofs of payment, social media posts, photos, and so on) without a proper foundation unless the opposing litigant or lawyer objects.
Custody and Domestic Violence
https://www.womenslaw.org/.../custody-and-domestic-violence
Brief overview of the way domestic violence intersects with custody cases. We discuss how judges might consider domestic violence when deciding custody, limits that can be put in place to protect the abused parent and child, and the relationship between custody cases and restraining orders.
Recording Phone Calls and Conversations: 50-State Survey
https://www.justia.com/.../recording-phone-calls-and.../
Federal and state laws differ as to the legality of recording phone calls and conversations. Determining which jurisdiction's law controls in cases involving recording devices or parties in multiple states can be complex, so it is likely best to adhere to the strictest applicable law when in doubt, and/or get the clear consent of all parties before recording.
How Do I Find a Lawyer?
https://www.americanbar.org/.../how-do-i-find-a-lawyer-/
You've thought about it carefully and you've decided that you need to contact a lawyer. The big problem is—how to find one? This section will give you some tips on what to look for when choosing a lawyer, and lead you through some questions you can ask a lawyer when you first meet. If you do your homework, you can hire the lawyer who has the experience and expertise to help you with your problem.

Co-parenting Arrangement Without Going Through the Courts?
https://www.2houses.com/.../co-parenting-arrangement...
An amicable, voluntary agreement can help save time and money for parents
who want joint custody of their children.
Here, we'll discuss various ways to make co-parenting agreements without going
through the courts. We'll also answer some common questions about co-
parenting.

What is a guardian ad litem (GAL)?
https://www.custodyxchange.com/.../guardian-ad-litem.php
A guardian ad litem is a lawyer, a volunteer or a mental health professional who
determines the child's needs, then works to ensure their best interests are
upheld in court. They're tasked with conducting an investigation to figure out
what custody situation best suits the child, and whether protections like
supervised visitation are necessary.

Joint vs. Sole Custody
https://www.justia.com/.../child.../joint-vs-sole-custody/
Many people consider custody to be the right to control the physical location of
a child. Custody is multi-faceted, however, and encompasses both physical
custody, which is the right to determine where the child resides, and legal
custody, which is the right to make significant decisions regarding the child's
health, upbringing, and education.

Paternity Laws and Forms: 50-State Survey
https://www.justia.com/.../paternity-forms-50-state.../
Paternity is the process of determining the legal father of a child. This
designation may seem symbolic, but it has practical implications.
What You Should Know About Visitation Rights and the Law
https://www.familylawrights.net/.../is-withholding.../

One Mom's Battle
https://www.onemomsbattle.com/
The mission at One Mom's Battle is to raise awareness and educate family court
professionals on post separation abuse as it relates to co-parenting and the
family court system (divorce, paternity and child custody battles). Education on
high-conflict individuals and post separation abuse will allow family court
professionals (Judges, Commissioners, Magistrates, CPS workers, Guardian ad
Litems (GAL), Parenting Coordinators (PC), Custody Evaluators, therapists and
attorneys) to recognize the abusive dynamics that play out in the family court
system so they can make decisions that are in the best interest of children.

DOMESTIC VIOLENCE RESOURCES

National Network To End Domestic Violence
https://www.techsafety.org/seekinghelponline...
For a list of national hotlines that include phone, text or chat options
Path to Safety: National Domestic Violence Hotline
https://www.thehotline.org/help/path-to-safety/...
Interactive Guide to Safety Planning:
https://www.loveisrespect.org/
Forms of Abuse: The National Network to End Domestic Violence
https://nnedv.org/content/forms-of-abuse/
Signs of Relationship Abuse: UN Women
https://www.unwomen.org/.../infographic-signs...
National Domestic Violence Hotline
www.thehotline.org
1-800-799-SAFE (7233)
RAINN National Sexual Assault Hotline
https://www.rainn.org/
1-800-656-4673
Global Network of Women's Shelters
https://gnws.org/
Women'sLaw.org
https://www.womenslaw.org/
Click on your state (in the map or in the drop-down menu) to find contact
information for 1) advocates in local domestic violence programs and shelters;
2) legal assistance organizations; 3) courthouse locations where you can file for a
protection order; and 4) sheriff departments. If you need to talk to someone
about an abusive relationship, you can call the National Domestic Violence
Hotline at 1-800-799-7233.

<h1 style="text-align:center">EDUCATION RESOURCES</h1>

Best Online Colleges 2023

https://thebestschools.org/rankings/online-colleges/
Online colleges have grown in number in the last decade, with many top colleges and state universities now offering distance education through online degrees. Unlike the perception just a few years ago, today, many graduates of accredited online colleges report high satisfaction with their choice to earn a degree online. Online programs provide a great alternative, allowing anyone to earn a degree that meets their goals in a flexible, affordable format – it's portable education!

Federal Student Aid

https://studentaid.ed.gov/sa/...
Start preparing for college by defining your goals and interests, understanding college costs, and planning financially and academically. Use the Free Application for Federal Student Aid (FAFSA®) form to apply for financial aid for college or grad school. Financial aid is money to help pay for college or career school. Grants, work-study, loans, and scholarships help make college or career school affordable. Find the right repayment plan for you, learn how to make payments, get help if you can't afford your payments, and see what circumstances might result in a loan being forgiven, canceled, or discharged.

College Scholarships and Grants for Single Mothers

http://www.collegescholarships.org/grants/single-mothers.htm
Considering how much it costs to raise a family, single mothers looking to go to college need financial aid. Luckily, countless organizations recognize that single parents need help paying for school. That is why a lot of college scholarships and grants were created specifically for single mothers. These scholarships help single moms afford the education they need to create a secure financial future for themselves and their children.

Fastweb: Scholarships, Grants, Internships, & More

https://www.fastweb.com/ppc?utm_source=google...
For over 28 years, we have worked to help students discover scholarships that are targeted to their strengths, interests and skills. We also assist students in discovering the right college for their budget, making tough financial aid decisions and finding internship opportunities that will help them bridge the divide between college and post-graduate life. Finally, we give students the option to pay for college with part-time jobs by offering part time job search and advice.

Bank of America Institute for Women's Entrepreneurship at Cornell

https://bofainstitute.cornell.edu

The new Bank of America Institute for Women's Entrepreneurship at Cornell offers an unparalleled opportunity for women to earn a certificate in business from this Ivy League university. Through a free online program made possible by Bank of America, students will gain the skills, knowledge and resources necessary to build, manage and scale a successful business.

Guide to Choosing College Majors

https://blog.collegeboard.org/the-ultimate-guide-to...

We know that choosing a college major can be overwhelming. But have no fear! Your choice of major will not lock you into a specific career for the rest of your life. That said, you WILL spend a lot of time whatever subject you choose. Here's what you need to know about college majors before you commit.

Alison: Free Online Courses

https://alison.com/

Alison offers over 4000 free online courses across nine distinct categories. The types of courses across the categories include:

Certificate Courses, and Diploma Courses

Benefits.gov

https://www.benefits.gov/.../U.S.%20Department%20of...

Find and apply for a variety of education and training benefits.

Chegg

https://www.chegg.com/

Purchase or rent textbooks and save up to 90%. Get help with homework, assistance is offered 24/7. You can even look into different colleges and browse internship opportunities.

Coursera

https://www.coursera.org/

This is one of the most valuable learning resources on the web. Students can find free courses provided by prestigious universities. Almost all courses are offered, including humanities, computer science, business, mathematics, biology, and more. This website is necessary for all students who want to expand their knowledge on a subject or find information they will use for their school projects.

Saylor

https://www.saylor.org/...

Saylor Academy is a nonprofit initiative working since 2008 to offer free and open online courses to all who want to learn. We offer nearly 100 full-length courses at the college and professional levels, each of which is available right now — at your pace, on your schedule, and free of cost.

PCs for People

https://pcsrefurbished.com/sales/categorySales.aspx...
Since 1998, PCs for People has been a driving force behind digital inclusion efforts across the US. As a 501(c)(3) non-profit organization, our mission is to provide a bridge across the digital divide that offers employment and educational opportunities to low-income individuals, families with children, and those with disabilities.

Laptops 4 Learning

https://laptops4learning.videoscholarship.org/
Since 2015, Laptops 4 Learning, a 501(c)(3) non-profit has provided hundreds of laptops to low income students to pursue online education.

Guide to Going Back to School as an Adult

https://study.com/res.../adult-learners-returning-to-college
Returning to school as an adult can open up a new world of possibilities. This guide details the college application process, how to get college credit for work experience, tips for school and work balance, and scholarships for adult learners.

Earn College Credits with CLEP Exams

https://clep.collegeboard.org/?
ef_id=Cj0KCQiAx6ugBhCcARIsAGNmMbj1MLi4lRWP531RGX8xw9iriPivpfkbUz70cGJvSIcTY
s30wM4RhBEaAmniEALw_wcB:G:s&s_kwcid=AL!4330!3!616208518311!e!!g!!clep%20exa
ms!1493550655!572490017003&gclid=Cj0KCQiAx6ugBhCcARIsAGNmMbj1MLi4lRWP531R
GX8xw9iriPivpfkbUz70cGJvSIcTYs30wM4RhBEaAmniEALw_wcB
CLEP exams let you test out of introductory courses and move to more advanced courses sooner, saving time toward your degree.

Custody Xchange Single Parent Scholarships

https://www.custodyxchange.com/scholarships/
The Custody X Change Giving Fund awards three scholarships worldwide to single parents each year for undergraduate study.

The Graduate Network

https://graduate-network.org/
This is an affiliation of school, government organizations, businesses, non-profits and college graduates, all working together to help support adults who are returning to college to complete a degree. This network provides connections to employers, access to tuition benefits and connections to local, city and state support groups for the 37 million 'Comebackers' in this country -- students with some college credits but no degree.

Massive Open Online Courses

https://www.mooc.org/
Massive Open Online Courses (MOOCs) are free online courses available for anyone to enroll. MOOCs provide an affordable and flexible way to learn new skills, advance your career and deliver quality educational experiences at scale.

EMPLOYMENT & RESUME RESOURCES

We often see members ask about updating or building their resumes or seeking insight into various career fields. We have compiled a list of different resources and articles with links and descriptions to help guide you on your path.

Dress for Success

https://dressforsuccess.org/

Dress for Success is a global not-for-profit organization that empowers women to achieve economic independence by providing a network of support, professional attire and the development tools to help women thrive in work and in life.

How to Write a Resume

https://how-to-write-a-resume.org

The mission of How To Write A Resume.org is to assist job hunters in their job search by producing and distributing a winning cover letter and resume. On the site we have included free tips for resume writing, cover letter suggestions and interviewing tips and tools to land the perfect job. Please let us know if you have any questions or suggestions for the site.

CareerOnestop

https://www.careeronestop.org/

Explore careers, find training, and search for jobs. The site offers free online career tools, tips and information, and links to local services.

Glassdoor

https://www.glassdoor.com/index.htm

Glassdoor offers millions of the latest job listings, combined with a growing database of company reviews, CEO approval ratings, salary reports, interview reviews and questions, benefits reviews, office photos and more.

How to Prepare for an Interview

https://www.indeed.com/.../how-to-prepare-for-an-interview

Preparing for an interview might seem intimidating, but there are several steps you can take to prepare yourself for a successful interview.

Seven Tips for Reentering the Workforce

https://www.monster.com/career.../article/going-back-to-work

The Mom Project

https://work.themomproject.com/talentsignup...

Through our job board, you can find opportunities at companies that value your talent—and make sure you have the freedom you need to be there for your family. Search for full-time, part-time, remote, and freelance jobs.

Unemployment Help

https://www.usa.gov/unemployment

Learn how to apply for unemployment benefits, workers' compensation, welfare or temporary assistance, and other programs and services that can help if you lose your job.

FlexJobs
https://www.flexjobs.com/
Work is changing, and remote and hybrid jobs are becoming a new normal.
Now, "the office" is often a home office, hybrid workplace, or wherever you want
to set up shop. As the #1 job site to find the best remote, work from home, and
flexible jobs for over 14 years, we know how to help you have a faster, easier,
and safer job search. Just as we've helped millions of people, let us help you!

Amazon Jobs
https://www.amazon.jobs/en/location/virtual-locations
Amazon has virtual (or "remote") positions available to qualified individuals who
live in some areas. So if you aren't near a physical Amazon location, or just want
to see if there are virtual opportunities in your area, you're in the right place.

Live Career
https://www.livecareer.com/
Online resume building, with help translating skills from one field to another.
Create your own and learn from examples. Recruiter-approved career tools to
help you land the job. From engineering to dentistry to finance, our
professionally written resume examples are tailored to thousands of unique job
titles.

15 Work-From-Home Jobs for Single Parents
https://www.indeed.com/.../single-mom-working-from-home

Parenting as a Remote Worker
https://about.gitlab.com/.../cul.../all-remote/parenting/...
Creative Strategies from Single Parents on Juggling Work and Family
https://hbr.org/.../creative-strategies-from-single...
A survival guide to working from home as a single parent
https://www.standard.co.uk/.../working-from-home-kids...

Hire My Mom
https://www.hiremymom.com/
HireMyMom is on a mission to make the hiring process easier and more
affordable by connecting small businesses directly to talented remote workers.

Childcare .gov
https://childcare.gov/consumer.../if-you-cant-find-care
Having trouble finding child care even after looking for a while? Read on for
ideas about what to do if you have not yet been able to find the right child care
option for your family.

LinkedIn
https://about.linkedin.com
Welcome to LinkedIn, the world's largest professional network with 810 million
members in more than 200 countries and territories worldwide.

PhotoFeeler

https://www.photofeeler.com

Test Your Photo For Business, Social, & Dating

To choose your best pics, get objective feedback in a respectful, moderated environment. Target voters by gender and age.

Path Forward

https://pathforward.org/

Looking to restart your career after caregiving? Path Forward offers returning professionals the opportunity to return to work at companies that appreciate the skills they offer, the perspective they provide, and the contributions they can make.

ReachHire

https://www.reachire.com/

We believe in partnering with leading employers who recognize professionals' skills and experience – not their career breaks – and are committed to creating more career off-ramps and on-ramps, and building concrete paths to leadership for women.

The Second Shift

https://www.thesecondshift.com/

We represent a vetted network of the most experienced female talent around, and we take a full-service approach to helping companies maximize their expertise.

How to Navigate Illegal Interview Questions While on the Job Hunt

https://theriveter.co/.../how-to-navigate-illegal.../

Single Mom Jobs Network

https://singlemomjobsnetwork.com/

The Single Mom Jobs Network is a website developed to assist in connecting single moms with flexible employment opportunities, career coaching services well as career tools and business resources to help mothers to be successful in their personal lives.

Work 180

https://work180.com/en-us/about-us/our-story

We empower women with the information they need to choose workplaces that work for them. At the heart of this revolution is our transparent job board.

Wealthy Single Mommy: Best 28 jobs for single moms in 2023

https://www.wealthysinglemommy.com/jobs-for-single-moms/

Top 40 Work-From-Home Companies for Remote Jobs in 2023
https://www.indeed.com/.../best-work-from-home-companies
In this article, we've compiled a list of the 40 best work-from-home companies
that have an Indeed company rating of at least four out of five stars.
26 In-Demand Jobs You Can Do From Home or Remote Sites
https://www.indeed.com/.../finding-a.../jobs-to-do-from-home
LinkedIn
https://www.linkedin.com/
The mission of LinkedIn is simple: connect the world's professionals to make
them more productive and successful
Indeed Career Services & Employment Opportunities
https://www.indeed.com/m/
Career Services through Indeed can provide you with the toolkit needed to craft
a compelling resume. Writing and updating your resume can feel overwhelming,
but help is here. Indeed offers multiple services that vary in level of assistance.
Upwork Freelancing
https://www.upwork.com/
Search on Talent Marketplace™ for the hourly or fixed-price work you're looking
for. Submit a proposal, set your rate, and show how great you'll be. Give a little
extra by sharing your unique approach and offering a rapport-building
interview.

WAYS TO EARN EXTRA INCOME

Become a notary

These individuals are independent contractors who earn money by handling mortgage signings, notarizing trust documents and performing many other tasks.

Taskrabbit Tasker

https://www.taskrabbit.com/become-a-tasker

TaskRabbit connects busy people in need of help with trusted local Taskers who can lend a hand with everything from home repairs to errands. As a Tasker, you can get paid to do what you love, when and where you want — all while saving the day for someone in your city.

Offer Pet Services on Rover

https://www.rover.com/become-a-sitter/

Boarding-Care for a dog or cat overnight in your home. Sitters who offer boarding can make up to 2x more than sitters who don't.

Dog Walking-Pick up dog walks that fit your schedule.

Doggy Day Care-Ideal for work-from-home dog lovers.

House Sitting, Drop-In Visits-Stay with or check up on pets in their own homes.

Become a Caregiver

Caregivers can create a profile online that outlines their skills, experience and the price that they charge for their services such as,

-Babysitters

-Senior care

-Pet care

-Housekeeping

-Daycare

-Tutoring

Care

https://www.care.com/

Sittercity

https://www.sittercity.com/sitter/account

Urban Sitter

https://www.urbansitter.com/signup/sitter

Tutor .com

https://www.tutor.com/apply

Affiliate Marketing
The process of promoting someone else's products or services and making a commission whenever someone buys after clicking your affiliate link.
For example, if you publish a blog post or a YouTube video sharing the best vacuum cleaners for pet hair and someone buys a product you recommend after clicking your affiliate link, you get paid a percentage of that sale.
Beginner's Guide
https://ahrefs.com/blog/affiliate-marketing/
50+ of the Best Affiliate Programs That Pay the Highest Commission
https://blog.hubspot.com/marketing/best-affiliate-programs
E-Commerce/Dropshipping
What is E-Commerce Dropshipping?
E-commerce dropshipping is a business model where you, as a seller, can sell items without keeping them in stock. Instead, you partner up with manufacturers who ship items directly to the customers who place orders through your website.
Beginners Guide
https://www.nexcess.net/blog/dropshipping-vs-ecommerce/
Freelance
Freelancing is a type of self-employment. Instead of being employed by a company, freelancers tend to work as self-employed, delivering their services on a contract or project basis.
-Writing
-Content Marketing
-Copyrighting
-Blog Editing
-Web Design/Development
-Graphic Design
-Social Media Management
-Virtual Assistant
-Translation
-Photography
& any other skill you have that may help.
Best Sites to Market Your Services
https://www.business.com/.../10-top-sites-for-freelance.../

Ridesharing
11 Things To Know Before Becoming An Uber Or Lyft Driver
https://www.forbes.com/.../11-things-to-know-before.../amp/
Uber: Drive or Deliver
https://www.uber.com/us/en/drive/
Lyft
https://www.lyft.com/driver-application-requirements
Delivery Services
10 Best Paying Delivery Jobs
https://www.indeed.com/.../find.../best-paying-delivery-jobs
Online Focus Groups
Focus groups can be a lucrative side hustle when you break down per-hour pay. You get to be a part of a company's market research efforts, magnifying your opinion above those of other potential consumers.
8 Paid Focus Group Opportunities
https://gigworker.com/paid-focus-groups/
Mystery Shopping
Mystery shoppers make an impact in their local communities by helping stores, restaurants, and banks become better places for consumers like you to visit.
Sinclair Customer Metrics
https://www.sinclaircustomermetrics.com/Mystery_Shopping...
Market Force Information
https://www.marketforce.com/become-a-shopper...
IntelliShop
https://intelli-shop.com/shopper-hub
Elite CXS
https://elitecxs.com/become-an-elite-shopper/
Mystery Shopping Service
https://www.mysteryshoppingservice.com/shoppers/

Teach English Online
From the comfort of your living room, or kitchen, you can almost teach from anywhere in the world as long as you meet our basic requirements. No need to hop on that commuter bus since everything is online.
VIPkid
https://m.vipkid.com/teach/teacher-requirements
Transcription
A transcriptionist is someone who listens to an audio or video recording and then types everything that is said with accuracy and provides a clean document free of spelling, grammar and punctuation errors. Some transcription companies require a level of accuracy right down to every "uh" and "um," so it's important to have excellent attention to detail in this job. Some of the things you may be asked to transcribe include podcasts, interviews, business meetings and classroom lectures.
24 Online Transcription Jobs for Beginners (With Rate Info)
https://www.indeed.com/.../find.../online-transcription-jobs
App and Website Testing
As a website tester, your job is to test and evaluate the performance of a site on the internet. In this role, you pretend to be a normal user, consider the design and usability of the site on your computer, and provide feedback on the site's performance.
30 Best Sites Where You Can Test Websites for Money (2023)
https://logicaldollar.com/test-websites-for-money/
Earn Cash Back on Purchases
Sell Used Clothing or Unused Items
Test and Review Products
Get Paid to Test and Review Products at Home Free in 2023
https://www.productreviewmom.com/.../how-can-i-get-paid...

HOUSING, SHELTERS, & UTILITIES RESOURCES

NACA
https://www.naca.com/
We're committed to helping the underserved build generational wealth through access to affordable mortgages and financial assistance.
HUD: Housing Counseling Services
https://hudgov-answers.force.com/housingcounseling/s/...
The nationwide network of HUD participating housing counseling agencies have been helping consumers across America for more than 50 years by providing the answers they need to make informed housing decisions.
Rental Assistance
https://www.hud.gov/topics/rental_assistance
Housing Choice Voucher Program
https://www.hud.gov/.../housing_choice_voucher_program...
HUD: Buying a Home
https://www.hud.gov/topics/buying_a_home
Thinking about buying a home? We have information that can help! Got questions? Talk to one of our housing counselors!
Foreclosure Avoidance Counseling
https://apps.hud.gov/offices/hsg/sfh/hcc/fc/index.cfm
Emergency Rental Assistance Programs
https://home.treasury.gov/.../emergency-rental-assistance...
To meet this need, the Emergency Rental Assistance program makes funding available to assist households that are unable to pay rent or utilities.
Find rental assistance programs in your area
https://www.consumerfinance.gov/.../find-help-with-rent.../
What to do if you're facing eviction
https://www.consumerfinance.gov/.../what-to-do-if-youre.../
If you're behind on rent and received a demand for payment, an eviction notice, or an eviction lawsuit, you're in the right place.
We can help you understand your rights and how to take advantage of federal and state help.

Loveline

https://loveline.com/need-help/

Our goal at LoveLine is to connect with you and actively listen to hear your needs. We will start by getting to know you when you contact us by phone call, chat or through referral. We will commit to care for you and follow through to ensure your most critical needs are met first. We will provide you with ongoing support in your own community through loving volunteers and organizations that we have a relationship with.

Homeless Assistance

https://www.hud.gov/findshelter

If you are at risk of being homeless or in need of transitional housing, HUD partners may be able to work with you on a long-term plan and connect you with resources for success.

Low Income Home Energy Assistance Program (LIHEAP)

https://www.benefits.gov/benefit/623

Assists eligible low-income households with their heating and cooling energy costs, bill payment assistance, energy crisis assistance, weatherization and energy-related home repairs.

Just Shelter

https://justshelter.org/community-resources/

Across America there are hundreds of organizations working hard to preserve affordable housing, prevent eviction, and reduce family homelessness. Click on the map to search over 600 organizations

National Council of State Housing Agencies (NCSHA)

https://www.ncsha.org/housing-help/

Housing Finance Agencies offer individuals, families, and businesses a wide range of support and assistance. Click your state to find HFAs and organizations near you that can help you with your housing finance questions and concerns.

Affordable Housing Online

https://affordablehousingonline.com/

Affordable Housing Online has served low income renters in the U.S. for more than 15 years with the most complete and up-to-date info on low income housing, affordable housing, affordable apartments, subsidized housing, Public Housing and Section 8 Housing Choice Voucher (HCV) waiting list information. We provide current data on more than 77,500 apartment communities containing more than 6,229,000 apartment homes. We also provide detailed information about 4,058 local Public Housing Authorities (PHA) with housing authority contact, program, and current waiting list information - including instructions on how to apply for waiting lists and complete housing applications.

Local Home Buying Programs

https://www.hud.gov/buying/localbuying

In addition to HUD's mortgage insurance programs, there may be programs sponsored by your state or local government or other organizations. Select the state that interests you.

United Way 211

Dial 211 or visit https://www.211.org/services/essential-needs

Whether you need help finding emergency shelter, avoid homelessness, or find help staying in your home.

Habitat for Humanity

https://www.habitat.org/housing-help/apply

Habitat homeowners must be active participants in building a better home and future for themselves and their families. Every Habitat home is an investment. For us, it is one answer to a critical need, and we believe that stronger homes will create stronger communities.

Salvation Army - Energy Assistance Programs

https://centralusa.salvationarmy.org/usc/utility_assistance/

By providing a variety of services to help families and individuals weather the storm, whether it be financial emergency, shut-off notices or through a multitude of other hardships, every year we serve millions of individuals across the United States.

Tenant Rights by State

https://www.hud.gov/topics/rental_assistance/tenantrights

CoAbode

https://www.coabode.org/

CoAbode is the next generation of social networking, taking interaction off the screen and into day to day life. We match people for home-sharing based on personality, what each person values, and for community building at every stage of life, building stable homes, shared child care and stability in uncertain times. Real life social connection and home-sharing builds health and well-being and millions of Americans can benefit from our approach to community building through CoAbode.

Co-parenting Styles, Plans & Communication Resources

State Child Support Calculators

https://www.alllaw.com/calculators/childsupport

Each state has it's own statutory guidelines that judges use to determine the amount of monthly child support paid by the non-custodial parent. Link provides guidelines for each.

Co-Parenting Communication Guide

https://www.afccnet.org/Portals/0/PDF/AzAFCC%20Coparenting%20Communication%20Guide-web.pdf?ver=RHuPIAndBbyj90inSgT2Xg%3d%3d

On a regular and ongoing basis, co-parents will need to exchange information about their child(ren). This guide provides tools, tips and good practices for co-parents to follow to communicate with one another.

A Brief Guide to Family Mediation for Parents Who Are Self-Represented

https://www.afccnet.org/Portals/0/PDF/Representing%20Yourself%20Mediation.pdf?ver=H_EHSdrl8yMC2zse9QziKA%3d%3d

How to Make Your Parenting Plan or Agreement

https://www.custodyxchange.com/.../ove.../parenting-plan.php

Your parenting plan or custody agreement outlines how you and the other parent will continue to care and provide for your children after you separate. An effective plan is personalized to fit the needs of your family situation and contains the following information.

What Is Parallel Parenting? Plus, Creating a Plan That Works

https://www.healthline.com/.../parenting/parallel-parenting

If there's a lot of hurt, anger, grief, and resentment between two people, constantly seeing each other can open old wounds and cause conflict. If you find yourself in this situation, you may want to try a strategy called parallel parenting to keep the situation amicable — or at least tolerable.

Talking Parents: Free Co-Parenting Communication Tools

https://talkingparents.com/home

Talking Parents is the free and fully secure co-parenting communication tool. We help co-parents communicate and avoid disputes by maintaining an unalterable record of all conversations, important dates, and shared files.

Our Family Wizard

https://www.ourfamilywizard.com/

Families around the world are choosing OFW® to manage shared custody, joint custody and parenting plans. OFW® is recommended by courts in all 50 states as a tool to manage shared parenting communication. OFW® Professional Access keeps your family law and mental health practitioners informed in real-time.

Legal Services Corporation
https://www.lsc.gov/
LSC is the single largest funder of civil legal aid for low-income Americans in the nation. Established in 1974, LSC operates as an independent 501(c)(3) nonprofit corporation that promotes equal access to justice and provides grants for high-quality civil legal assistance to low-income Americans. LSC distributes more than 90 percent of its total funding to 132 independent nonprofit legal aid programs with more than 800 offices.

Up to Parents - Free Online Workshop & Co-Parenting Info
https://www.uptoparents.org/Default.aspx
Online educational tool for parents raising children between two homes. This resource has already assisted over 250,000 parents in building a focus on their children's needs—and then using that focus to define and guide their future interaction.

The Coparenting Collective
https://www.thecoparentingcollective.com/
An Exclusive Community & Podcast for Separated Parents and Blended Families
BOOK: The Co-Parenting Survival Guide: Letting Go of Conflict After a Difficult **Divorce**
https://a.co/d/5kUq7wC

BOOK: Joint Custody with a Jerk: Raising a Child with an Uncooperative Ex-A Hands-on, Practical Guide to Communicating with a Difficult Ex-Spouse
https://a.co/d/bM7hKZO

BOOK: The Co-Parents' Handbook: Raising Well-Adjusted, Resilient, and Resourceful Kids in a Two-Home Family from Little Ones to Young Adults
https://a.co/d/9C53JzN

NOLO
https://www.nolo.com/
Nolo has an extensive library of legal articles—all for free. The law can be hard to find, complex, and intimidating. We strive to make it accessible to everyone—to help people find answers to their everyday legal and business questions.

LawHelp
https://www.lawhelp.org
LawHelp helps people of low and moderate incomes find free legal aid programs in their communities, answers to questions about their legal rights and forms to help them with their legal problems.

SplitSmart

https://splitsmart.com

SplitSmart is an online divorce tool to help couples organize financial and child issues so they can avoid most divorce expense and drama. Our tool focuses on the human side of divorce to get couples organized so they can quickly reach an agreement with minimal expense. SplitSmart provides couples with a: marital worksheet, co-parenting plan, and an alternative approach to child support.

The Cooperative Parenting Institute

https://cooperativeparenting.com

Focused on providing services, education, and products to high conflict families.

Medical News Today: What is Gray Rocking?

https://www.medicalnewstoday.com/articles/grey-rock

Gray rocking, or the grey rock method, is a tactic some people use when dealing with abusive or manipulative behavior.

7 Strategies to Overcome Conflict in Co-Parenting

https://www.ourfamilywizard.com/.../7-strategies-overcome...

Mended Families: Types of Coparenting

https://mended-families.com/.../spoiler-alert-there-are.../

The Ins and Outs of Co-Parenting Counseling

https://www.mcmorrowlaw.com/.../the-ins-and-outs-of-co.../

The goal of co-parenting counseling is to improve parenting relationships by reducing conflict and improving communication, ultimately protecting and improving the overall well-being of the children involved.

Implementing Yellow Rock Communication When Co-Parenting with a Narcissist

https://www.onemomsbattle.com/.../implementing-yellow...

The yellow rock method is a spin on the gray rock method. It involves adding some niceties to gray rock communication.

New and Expecting Mom Resources
The Special Supplemental Nutrition Assistance Program for Women, Infants and Children (WIC)
https://www.fns.usda.gov/wic
provides federal grants to states for supplemental foods, health care referrals, and nutrition education for low-income pregnant, breastfeeding, and non-breastfeeding postpartum women, and to infants and children up to age five who are found to be at nutritional risk.

Pregnancy Tracking
How big is your baby? What is happening this week? Use one (or all!) of the following apps to keep track of your developing baby: Ovia, Glow Nurture, Baby Bump, Pregnancy+, Sprout, The Bump

Registry Rewards
Several stores and websites provide free samples and gifts if you create a Baby Registry with them. Examples include Amazon, Target, and Walmart.

Birth Plan Templates
https://www.thebump.com/a/tool-birth-plan
https://earthmamaorganics.com/pages/free-birth-plan
Birth plans help you and your care team stay on the same page when it comes to labor and delivery.

Evidence Based Birth
https://www.evidencebasedbirth.com
Evidence Based Birth® is an online childbirth resource that informs, empowers and inspires expecting parents and birth-care practitioners globally, to understand the latest, proven, evidence based care practices.

La Leche League International
https://www.llli.org
Their Mission is to help mothers worldwide to breastfeed through mother-to-mother support, encouragement, information, and education, and to promote a better understanding of breastfeeding as an important element in the healthy development of the baby and mother. Breastfeeding information and lactation support near you!

KellyMom
https://kellymom.com
Information on breastfeeding and parenting.

Aeroflow Breastpumps
https://www.aeroflowbreastpumps.com
Qualify for a free or low-cost breast pump through your insurance!

Human Milk 4 Human Babies
Need breastmilk? Have extra breastmilk to donate? The mission of Human Milk 4 Human Babies Global Network is to promote the nourishment of babies and children around the world with human milk. We are dedicated to fostering community between local families who have chosen to share breastmilk.

Formula Samples and Coupons
Register with Enfamil Family Beginnings and/or Similac StrongMoms to receive samples, coupons, and rewards for formula. https://www.enfamil.com/baby-formula-coupons-samples https://similac.com/strongmoms

Safe Kids
https://www.safekids.org/parents
Safe Kids Worldwide is a global organization working around the world to keep kids safe. Our partners work in 30 countries and in 400 coalitions throughout the United States. Learn about safety for kids, from car seats to choking.

National Diaper Bank Network
https://nationaldiaperbanknetwork.org/member-directory/
NDBN connects and supports the country's more than 200 community-based diaper banks that collect, store and distribute free diapers to struggling families. The Network serves nearly 280,000 children throughout the country each month.

Milestones
Is your child reaching their developmental milestones? Are you concerned your child is not "where they should be" for their age? Learn about developmental milestones and when to contact your child's doctor with the help of the CDC. There is a free app!

Babycenter
If you have ever Googled a mom/parent/baby-related topic, one of the top results was probably BabyCenter. It offers an astounding selection of information and resources, many written by doctors, nurses, and professionals.

MENTAL HEALTH RESOURCES

BetterHelp
https://www.betterhelp.com
Making professional therapy accessible, affordable, and convenient — so
anyone who struggles with life's challenges can get help, anytime and anywhere.
988 Suicide and Crisis Lifeline
https://www.988lifeline.org
The Lifeline provides 24/7, free and confidential support for people in distress,
prevention and crisis resources for you or your loved ones, and best practices
for professionals in the United States.
Text #988
National Alliance on Mental Illness (NAMI)
https://www.nami.org
NAMI provides advocacy, support, and education for individuals and families
affected by mental illness.
Substance Abuse and Mental Health Services Administration (SAMHSA)
https://ww.samhsa.gov
SAMHSA is a government agency that works to reduce the impact of substance
abuse and mental illness on America's communities by providing resources,
programs, and services.

SOCIAL MEDIA ORGANIZATIONS, BLOGGERS, PODCASTS, AND INFLUENCERS

The Single Mom Blog & The Single Mom Podcast were created by Heather Wells, a single mom of 3, as a resource for all single moms to find support, inspiration & more to help them through their single parent journey. Through blog posts, articles, podcast episodes, The Single Mom Blog & Podcast reminds all the single moms out there that they are not alone and that they are simply amazing!
Instagram username
thesinglemomblogger
Facebook Username
TheSingleMomBlogger
Website URL
https://www.thesinglemomblog.com
Lifestyle Tea Podcast is for single moms. I go over the ups,down and around experiences of a single mom. I also have bookclub vibes episodes on Monday.
Instagram username
lifestyletea_
Facebook Username
Lifestyle Tea Group
Meet Sonia, a determined single mother who refuses to let her challenges define her. With little to no available support, she uses motherhood as an opportunity to grow, not only as a parent but also as an individual. From scratch, Sonia pursued her education and has become a women's empowerment blogger, inspiring and motivating women to live their best lives.
Instagram username
@lifewithsoniablog
Twitter Username
lifewithsonia
Facebook Username
Lifewithsoniablog
Website URL
https://wwww.lifewithsonia.com
Author and creator of Singlenycmom.com, a blog that has lots of important information and resources for Single Moms but also filled with some fun stuff too fun. In my story section, I interview professionals such as Child Psychologists, on many valuable topics that will empower moms with the knowledge they need to be the best parent they can be.
Instagram username
@mtmcherry
Website URL
https://www.singlenycmom.com

ASANTE PUBLISHING

#CatchAFallingStar

www.ingramcontent.com/pod-product-compliance
Lightning Source LLC
Chambersburg PA
CBHW080256030726
47593CB00009B/2513